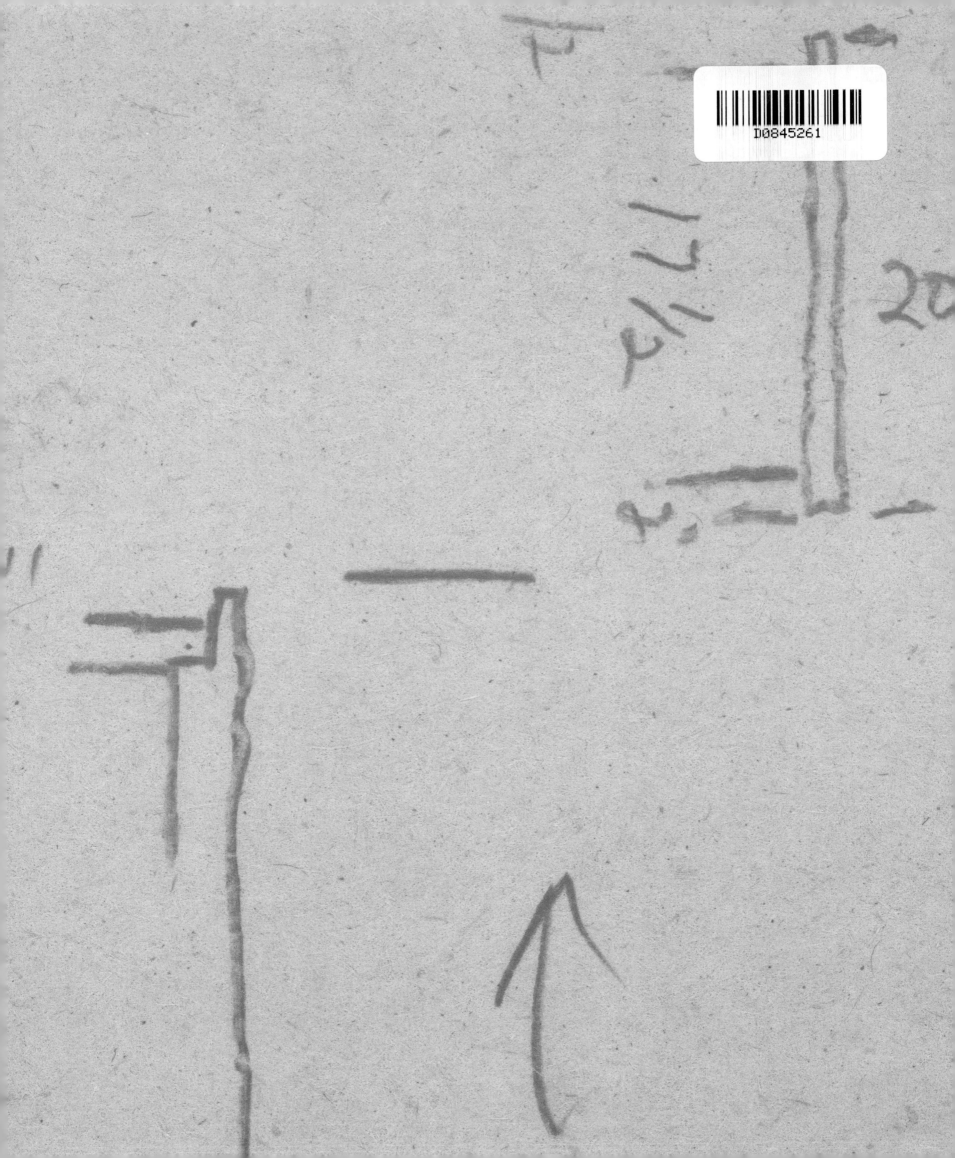

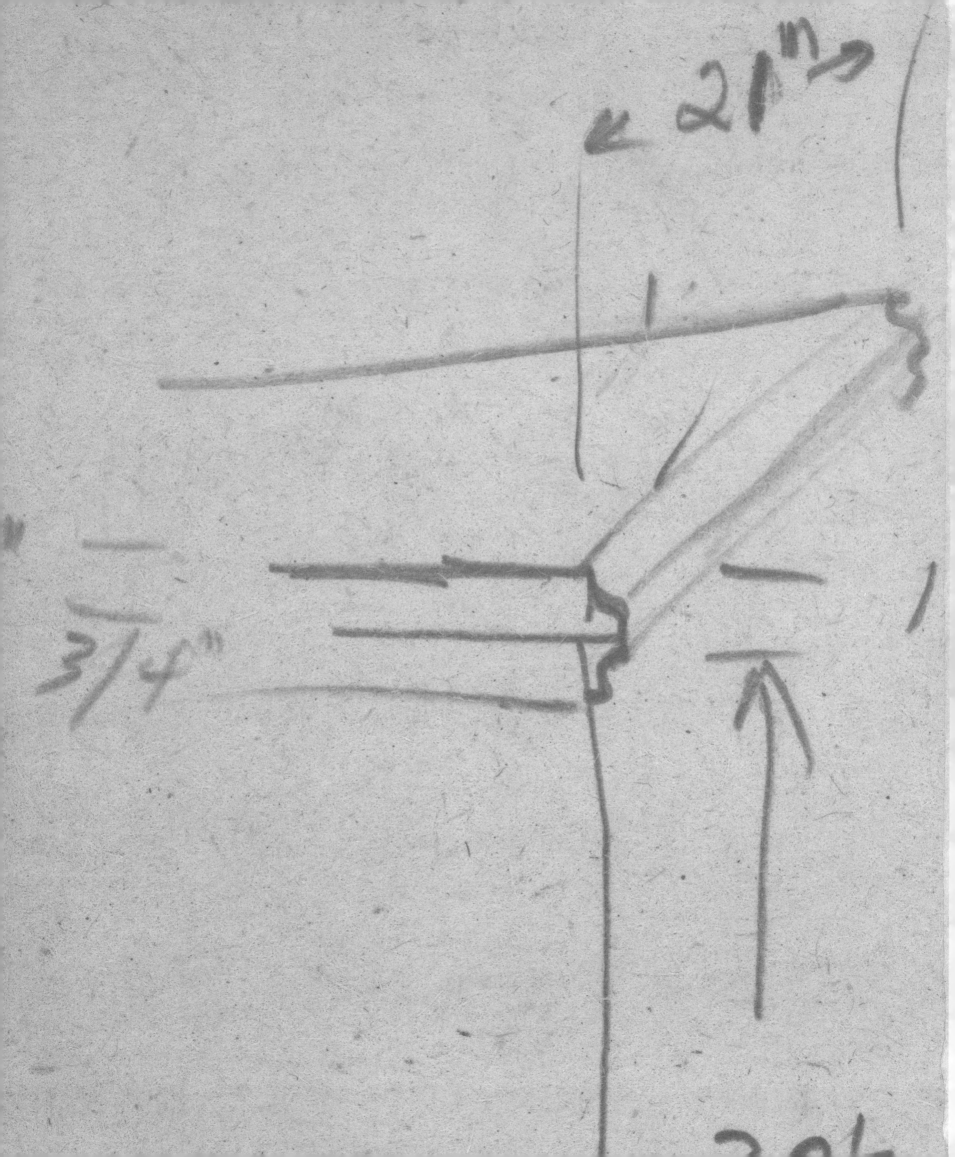

THOS.
MOSER

THOS. MOSER

ARTISTRY IN WOOD

BY THOMAS F. MOSER
WITH BRAD LEMLEY

FOREWORD BY ANDY ROONEY

CHRONICLE BOOKS

SAN FRANCISCO

Library of Congress Cataloging-in-Publication Data is available.

ISBN 0-8118-3611-8

Book and cover design:
Blue Design, Portland, Maine (www.bluedes.com)

Manufactured in China

Distributed in Canada by
Raincoast Books
9050 Shaughnessy Street
Vancouver, British Columbia V6P 6E5

10 9 8 7 6 5 4 3 2 1

Chronicle Books LLC
85 Second Street
San Francisco, California
94105

www.chroniclebooks.com

Pages 2–3: The former Los Angeles law office library of Baker and McKenzie; a
harmonious assemblage of vertical and horizontal lines.
Page 4: The arm is not attached to the back of the New Gloucester Rocker, allowing
each element to move independently. Where they touch, they often creak, giving
auditory pleasure along with physical comfort.
Opposite: A nascent designer may resent criticism offered by a more experienced
mentor, especially when he's the designer's father. However, while holding strong views,
David has been a willing, bright, and able design protégé.
Page 8: Squares on their way to becoming legs.
Page 10: High stools in the finishing room. Because each is hand-shaped and because
wood grain and color varies, no two are exactly alike.
Pages 12–13: Per Borre's Astral Bench is one of only three pieces in our history that
was built but not designed by us. With legs arrayed only along the exterior of a semi-
circle, it seems to defy gravity.

DEDICATION

To Paul Guilmette (1923–1979), whose encouragement and
steadfast faith in our future gave me the strength to make that
ninety degree turn all those years ago. Without him, there
would not have been this book or the enterprise
about which it is written.

CONTENTS

THOS. MOSER CABINETMAKERS
Auburn, Maine
1997
Kevin Owen

FOREWORD
by Andy Rooney

There are half a dozen truths so true that they come to my mind several times a week. One thing that's true is that the same things keep happening to the same people because of who they are and how they do things. There is a pattern of behavior, down to such minor matters as how we tie a shoelace, that determines the outcome of our lives. We are victims and beneficiaries of our strengths and weaknesses.

I write for a living and make furniture as a hobby, and it is depressing for me to be so often faced with the evidence that the things I do well and the things I do poorly are apparent in both my work and my hobby. They are not only apparent; they manifest themselves in everything I do for fun or money. I am, for example, invariably creative. Ideas come to me. They are often an unnecessary intrusion on the product, but originality is, generally speaking, a virtue so I'm pleased with myself for having it. But then I cannot follow any kind of direction or pattern. I am careless in execution. I start better than I finish. The results usually fall short of my vision of what they ought to be like. This is true of what I write and what I make of wood.

Opposite: After one year of employment, each Thos. Moser craftsman is qualified to sign furniture on its way to the finishing room. This privilege is taken very seriously and each piece is signed with great pride.

15

We met briefly, but I know Thomas Moser principally through his work. I therefore know him well. He couldn't surprise me with anything he did. He couldn't disappoint me because I am thoroughly familiar with his work and it reveals everything about him as a person.

In reading this book, I was pleased to have confirmed that long held belief that each of us does one thing basically the same way he or she does another. This book is proof that Thomas Moser does everything with the same care and originality with which he makes furniture. I had no intention of writing advertising copy here, and anyone reading this has probably already bought the book anyway, but I cannot resist saying how well done it is. It is too full of good things to be dismissed as a coffee table book. Dinner table, maybe.

In the summer of 1985, we were sailing with Walter Cronkite along the coast of Maine when a storm forced us into Boothbay Harbor, where Walter had the boat pulled for the duration of the three-day storm. In the course of our enforced shore leave we thought we had exhausted the cultural high points of the area, as well as its principle center of shopping interest, once we had spent several hours and a few hundred dollars at the L.L. Bean emporium.

Driving somewhat aimlessly around Portland, we noticed the sign THOS. MOSER CABINETMAKERS on a building that didn't appear to be a store. Over the years, catching sight of that sign has turned out to be a costly but rewarding observation. We parked, went in, and were immediately impressed with the display. My wife, Margie, was taken by the appearance and craftsmanship of a shaped cherry stool and cheerfully paid $400 for it.

Several months later we were all at a large party in a spacious New York apartment. The guests were more in number than anyone's dining table could accommodate so the hosts had used some ingenuity seating about thirty guests. I was at a billiard table that had been overlaid with a plywood top, and the seating, because of the height of the table, consisted of a random assortment of stools. Betsy Cronkite, seated next to me and remembering the Thos. Moser stool Margie had bought, turned and said, "Do you realize how much it would cost to seat these people if your wife supplied the stools?"

We have subsequently bought about a dozen other pieces of Thos. Moser's. Occasionally a guest in our home, having looked at furniture I made, will point to a Thos. Moser chair or table and say, "Did you make that, too?"

I resent the hint of awe in their voices that I had not detected when they were looking at one of my pieces, but I shuffle my feet, and say modestly, as though I could have made it if I wanted to, "No. I think Thomas Moser made that."

Andy Rooney is the regular commentator on 60 Minutes *and writes a newspaper column for the Tribune Media Services.*

Right: Andy Rooney in his home workshop as photographed by his daughter, Ellen Rooney (courtesy of *Fine Woodworking*). **Following pages:** Hand screws are woodworking clamps used to apply pressure to a glued joint. One never has too many.

Opposite: Essential to a round, oval, or bowfront table is the curved multi-laminate apron. Made up of ten or twelve layers, the outer layer is a continuous band of matching grain. Laminates are far stronger than steam-bends, so we prefer them for all but a few applications.
Above: As a college professor I wore a necktie (of sorts) in the mid-sixties. After the campus turmoil of the early seventies, ties were worn only by the "old guard" and administrators.

Chapter 1
ORIGINS

Some turning points are difficult to identify in retrospect, but not this one. I remember that cool September morning in 1971 as vividly as if it were yesterday. I was standing in the backyard of my house in New Gloucester, Maine, blinking in the brilliant summer sunshine, inspecting a table that I had just finished and brought up from my cellar workshop.

I am my own worst critic, but I have enough sense to know when I have done something well, and this was a good table. It had a five-foot-diameter round pine top, with one glue line down the middle. The top was made from a single board thirty-seven inches wide and sixteen feet long, one of six such boards from a first-growth Maine pine felled in 1922 (I still have the other five, and regard them as so precious that I can't bring myself to use them). The piece, with its robust, canted, turned ash legs, had the look of a rare eighteenth-century tavern table. Freshly finished with boiled linseed oil and hand-rubbed wax, it virtually glowed. Sue Vaughn, the wife of a friend, came by, saw the table, and offered to buy it on the spot.

It was just one moment in the dewy grass in rural Maine, but also an epiphany in the truest sense of the word. In an instant, at age thirty-six, I suddenly saw that there was enough artistry in me to produce something for which people would pay money. More importantly, those people would be getting their money's worth. In the evening, feeling my life teetering on the fulcrum of that moment, I said to my wife, Mary, "We could make a living building tables like this." I knew then that my ten-year career as a college professor would come to an end, my tenure evaporate, my pension shrivel, and my testimonial dinner remain forever uncooked. We had four children, little money, a big mortgage, and no particular reason to believe we could succeed, but I had almost no sense of choice at that time. I had to make things out of wood. It was as simple as that.

We did not formally begin the business for another year, but I mark that moment as the start of Thos. Moser Cabinetmakers, and of a thirty-year journey that has led to a place that I could not have imagined. The dingy two-hundred-square-foot basement shop in which I made that table has evolved into a sixty-five-thousand-square-foot, state-of-the-art facility that supplies furniture to showrooms in Maine, New York, Chicago, Charleston, and San Francisco. One lone woodworker has multiplied to sixty-five craftsmen whose works have been placed in every state and many countries, and who have influenced other designers both large and small. The aesthetic expression that impressed a friend years ago has, I believe, made some small difference in the world of modern furniture.

Skilled handwork is a family legacy. I was born in Chicago in 1935, and my father, Joseph, was a stereotyper, responsible for assembling and aligning the curved lead plates from which the *Chicago Tribune* was printed. This skill has long since been rendered obsolete by the computer, but at the time, his was a highly developed and demanding craft, requiring a meticulous touch to guarantee that all of the typographic elements were of the proper alignment and elevation. He was an artist in lead, a tradesman in the finest old-world sense.

Left: A passion to constantly learn new manual skills runs in the family. Sometime after World War I, my father, shown here, and his buddy, Red McGorty, bought a surplus JN-4 "Jenny" biplane from a pilot who gave each a single lesson. They kept the plane on the farm in Franksville, Wisconsin. They didn't have it long before Red landed on top of a barbed wire fence. Remnants of the propeller are still in the attic of the old farm house.
Opposite: Mert Leavitt owned a wood lot in Turner, Maine, and in the spring of 1976 he cut six thousand board feet of rock maple to sell. Since he worked for me, he gave me a good deal as only a Maine Yankee can. I still have some of that inventory.

"My father, who was not given to long speeches, did pass on one piece of advice: Buckle down. In other words, you get only one life, so don't fritter it away. Focus. Do something with it."

Both he and my mother, Sabina, were European immigrants. Joseph was Austrian and came here when he was seven years old; Sabina was German and emigrated at eighteen. From the time I was small, I had the sense of straddling the Old and New Worlds. My parents both spoke German in the home (I spoke it as a child; even today, I can speak what I call "five-year-old" German). Neither was schooled beyond the eighth grade, but they brought with them a prodigious, traditional European work ethic, and they reveled in the freedom to become so much more than the Old World would have allowed. I vividly remember my father being kidded by his brothers, Wisconsin farmers, who chided him for his city ways and ambition to improve himself. My mother was equally determined. Although she had been struck by a car on a Chicago street and walked with a serious limp, she was hardworking and frugal, and taught the family the value of deferred reward. My father, who was not given to long speeches, did pass on one piece of advice: Buckle down. In other words, you get only one life, so don't fritter it away. Focus. Do something with it.

My mother died of uterine cancer when she was forty-two, after she had suffered four years in great pain. I was fourteen. I am not sure what is the worst age to be when a parent dies, but fourteen, the age at which a child is rapidly transitioning to adulthood, must be close to it. She had been artistic, kind, stern, highly sympathetic, and loved me without reservation, so her death was a huge blow. My father worked nights, so my brother, Joseph Jr., two years my senior, and I more or less raised ourselves, and did not do a very good job of it. I performed poorly in school,

Opposite: Me (on left), Mother, and Brother, Joe. Yes, we wore knickers!
Right: In May 1958, I excavated for our little house in Geneseo, New York. We built every bit of it ourselves except for the concrete block foundation.

became alienated and angry, what I think of as an apprentice hoodlum. *Rebel Without a Cause* was playing at movie theaters then, and I saw myself in the James Dean character.

Yet the compulsion to build, to create something real and physical with my hands, was there from my earliest memory. I was always drawing and sketching on any paper I could find. I built a glider out of two-by-fours, and fell through a greenhouse as I attempted to glide from the garage roof to the backyard. Every kid had a scooter made of an old, separated roller skate nailed to an orange crate, but mine had to be painted, with a tin-can headlight and a mechanical brake. I built a Buck Rogers rocket, a semi-truck, and a roadster, in model scale and full size (that is, kid scale). This activity was constant; I could not stop myself.

I could not, and cannot to this day, imagine a life in which I am not creating objects in three dimensions. The urge runs deep in my bones, and for better or worse, I define myself by my output. The unexamined life may or may not be worth living, but for me, life without a project is a shallow experience.

The only high school course at which I excelled was mechanical drawing. Aside from that, I cut classes so often I was asked to withdraw from many of them. At the beginning of my senior year, I dropped out of high school.

My father died of pancreatic cancer when he was forty-nine, on my eighteenth birthday. Now, no remnant of "hearth" remained, and in an effort to find structure in a collapsed world, I joined the Air Force in April of the same year.

I spent much of my military service on guard duty in Greenland and Alaska, where there was nothing worth guarding and no one to guard against. After four unhappy years in uniform, I realized that I could forge

Left: My senior picture, class of 1960, State University of New York at Geneseo.
Opposite: We spent three years and more money than I care to remember adapting a five-axis router to form the rounded curve of the Continuous Arm Chair. After twenty-four years we still shape the arm entirely by hand using a rasp and sandpaper.

a future only through education. On the recommendation of a friend, I applied to and was accepted at the State University of New York at Geneseo, and I enrolled in January 1957. As the son of blue-collar immigrants and a high school dropout with abysmal grades, I impressed no one with my academic potential. The dean of students told me that he was admitting me because I was a veteran, and that I probably would not make it through the first semester.

I settled on speech education as a major, but it was the general liberal arts education that opened my eyes and touched my senses. For the first time in my life, I realized that I was as intelligent as the people around me. Although I took twenty-one hours of courses each semester and worked nights tuning pipe organs, I was never happier in my life. I felt a great sense of liberation, a release from the confines of superstition. I came to understand that every human phenomenon has a formulary, a thesis and antithesis, and I discovered books and experts and worlds that I'd had no idea existed. No day passed without a stunning revelation. I devoured each one.

Above: Air Police detail in Narsarssuak Air Base, Greenland, 1954. I'm at the far left.
Opposite: Our first house, Geneseo, New York; built entirely by us in the summer of 1958.

"A close friend once told me that, as opposed to the usual sequence of 'Ready! Aim! Fire!' the Tom Moser plan is typically 'Fire! Ready! Aim!'"

I married Mary Wilson during my freshman year. She had been my high school sweetheart in Chicago, and at my urging joined me in western New York state. We had known each other since I was fourteen and she was twelve, and she was and remains the most sympathetic and supportive person I have ever known.

We soon built a house. This undertaking exemplified a fundamental aspect of my personality, an aspect some might call confidence, and others, massive presumption. A close friend once told me that, as opposed to the usual sequence of "Ready! Aim! Fire!" the Tom Moser plan is typically "Fire! Ready! Aim!" At that point, the only boxlike structure I had ever built was a stereo-speaker enclosure. From that experience, I decided to build a house. On June 12, 1958, a truck disgorged a pile of lumber on the little lot we had purchased with part of the six thousand dollars I had inherited from my father and added to while in the Air Force. My only power tool was a saber saw. Mary, pregnant with our first child and working full-time at the University of Rochester, helped me at night, holding the light, handing me tools, and painting. I don't believe most American wives in 1958 would have submitted to such a regimen, but that summer of building became emblematic of our partnership, and the flame continues to burn bright after forty-five years.

Eighty days later, the house was habitable. I learned a lesson that  would serve me well: almost anything can be done if you break the project into its smallest pieces, and do those pieces one after another. If you can toenail a twelve-penny nail into a rafter, you can build a house, because a whole

"If you can toenail a twelve-penny nail into a rafter, you can build a house, because a whole house is simply a collection of achievements that are just that small and simple, piled one atop the other."

DENTILATION

PEDIMENT

TRIGLYPH

METOPE

house is simply a collection of achievements that are just that small and simple, piled one atop the other.

The process was joyous. I loved building that little house. The success primed me for more success; it paved the way for risk taking. The house still stands, a testament to youthful enthusiasm and an exercise in focused effort.

In 1958, I graduated with a bachelor's degree in speech education, and went on to graduate school at the University of Michigan, Ann Arbor, and at Cornell in Ithaca, New York. At the latter, I took the most wonderful course I have ever taken, in which we spent an entire semester on the aesthetics of the Parthenon. One building. The historical influence of it. The shape, the size, the resonances. To this day, I can tell anyone who cares to hear about triglyphs, metopes, entablatures, pediments, the Elgin marbles, and the use of lead in a joint.

The main thing that I learned from this and other design courses was that all architecture and furnishings have historical antecedents, and that

Opposite: Built in New Gloucester, Maine, in 1782 by Col. Isaac Parsons, his house stayed in his family until we bought it in 1967. Its classic simplicity inspired much of what we have created since. It really hurt when we had to sell it in the mid-1970s to keep the business afloat.
Right: Dhahran, Saudi Arabia—Mary and me after a three-week trek by Volkswagen bus through Kuwait, Iraq, and Southern Iran. We often navigated by compass alone.

the best design is incremental, constructed upon the accumulated wisdom of legions of designers and builders who have come before.

While in Ithaca, Mary and I also began an intense love affair with antiques. When people ask how I learned furniture design and woodworking, I always say that long-dead craftsmen taught me. To support our growing family—our first son, Matthew, was born in 1958—we purchased, fixed up, and sold antiques. We bought chairs off of front porches, desks out of barns, and even a truckload of parts from twenty-seven tall case clocks, part of the stock of a retired clock maker in Ann Arbor. I learned to scribe dovetails by reading 150-year-old tool marks on drawers. I learned to remove animal-hide glue with a heat gun, then melt it and use it again. I learned why buttermilk paint sticks and why it doesn't and how to liquefy it with straight ammonia, why some tenons loosen and others don't, and which woods are strongest in tension and which in compression. Upstate New York was the epicenter of nineteenth-century Greek and Roman revival architecture and furniture, and the pieces I was collecting coincided with the finest period in American woodworking, roughly 1845 to 1855. I was besotted with objects from that period: the dovetails, the pegged mortises and tenons, the beading, the fox wedges, the chamfers, the dadoes and rabbets and half-laps and finger joints, the delicate engineering of a Windsor chair that permitted twelve pounds of wood to provide secure seating for countless two-hundred-pound men for at least two hundred years.

I spent every evening and every weekend up to my elbows in those wonderful pieces. We would buy a bedraggled chair for twenty-five cents and sell it for twenty dollars, a battered pump organ for twenty dollars and sell it for two hundred dollars. One by one, I refurbished and sold each of those twenty-seven tall case clocks for as much as

Left: Mary and me at home in Geneseo, New York, over forty-four years ago.
Opposite: The most comfortable spindles are under tension. To achieve this curve, the holes in the arm and seat must be bored "out of alignment" at a predetermined angle.

six-hundred dollars apiece. Occasionally, I would make reproductions, sometimes for barter (I once traded a bookcase I built for a beat-up Studebaker). Mary set up a little antiques store called Riverside Antiques in our house. The G.I. Bill was played out and the inheritance money was long gone, so the store helped us to keep food on the table and me in graduate school.

Back then, in the 1960s, Mary and I felt isolated in our reverence for old things. From the end of the Great Depression and persisting well into the sixties and early seventies, this country was infected by a pervasive sense that old things were make-do and of no economic value. Antiques fashioned out of wood were not nearly as desirable as new, factory-produced objects made of chrome, aluminum, plastic, rayon, nylon, or plastic laminate. Handcrafts, when accorded any respect at all, were seen as strictly therapeutic, as things created by people who were depressed or stressed to make themselves feel better. In those days, you could buy a Stickley Morris chair for fifteen dollars; we owned several. I remember reading about the 1950s sale of a building full of Shaker chairs. The new owners piled them out back, tossed in a match, and burned them all. While reverence for old things never totally vanished—if it had, we could not have sold our refurbished antiques—we felt profoundly out of step with the 1960s Zeitgeist. Famed photographer and antiquarian Wallace Nutting was an early visionary. His 1929 *Furniture Treasury* was among the first written works to honor the beauty of early American furniture, and our copy is now dog-eared.

After receiving a Ph.D. in speech communication, I spent ten years teaching at several universities. I even taught for one year in Saudi Arabia, where I suffered from project-deficit syndrome, as I had almost nothing to do with my hands. Fortunately, I found a decrepit Volkswagen to overhaul and turn into a camper, and it saved my sanity. From Saudi Arabia, I moved the family to Maine. When Mary and I had been at Geneseo, we had taken a brief vacation in the state and fell in love with it and its culture.

Riverside Antiques

KELLOGG ROAD   R. D. 1
CORTLAND, NEW YORK

SK 3-3459   TOM AND MARY MOSER

Opposite: The Shakers were a strong influence on our early designs. Taken in the vestry in the early seventies.
Right: While I taught at the State University of New York at Cortland, Mary started an antique shop.

The resolute self-sufficiency of the people, the granite coast, the clapboard houses connected to barns, and the sense of time preserved and respected drew us powerfully. I was simultaneously offered a job teaching in Michigan for twelve thousand dollars a year and one at the University of Maine at Orono for eight thousand dollars. We took the Maine job in a heartbeat. I would have done it for much less.

In 1967, after a year at Orono, I accepted a job at Bates College in Lewiston, beginning a six-year career as an associate professor of speech. I taught communications, argumentation, persuasion, and rhetorical analysis, and I coached the debate team. On one level, it was one of the best times of my life. I felt blessed to have become a tenured college professor, and the intellectual stimulation was pure joy.

On another level, however, I grew increasingly restless with each passing year. My time at Bates coincided almost exactly with America's meltdown in Vietnam, and college campuses at the time were turbulent. Students and the general population were redefining education in ways I found profoundly disturbing. The predominant thinking was that course requirements were archaic. Grading was archaic. Sex-segregated dorms were archaic. Liberal arts education in general was archaic. By 1972, the core curriculum was replaced by so-called independent study, and the old ideals of what constitutes an educated person, ideals stretching back to ancient Greece—the ability to write, read, do mathematics, and create art—were suddenly a sexist, racist, repressive remnant of a dying culture. The operative term was "relevance." Aristotle had no relevance. Plato's *Republic* had no relevance. I had no relevance.

Other things began to worry me as well. There were professors all around me teaching off of yellowed notepads, dispensing rote lectures, and simply marking time until they could achieve retirement. As the

Opposite: Mary and I in Egypt in 1965 on our way to Saudi Arabia, where I taught English as a second language.
Right: Mary's passport photo with our little boys. We traveled as a family through the capitals of Europe and a big piece of the Middle East. No small adventure.

breadwinner for a large family, it would be easy to become entangled in that financially secure trap.

But most of all, I was increasingly dissatisfied with a career that did not involve working with my hands. Academics are kept people, the last aristocracy. Many of my colleagues were actually proud of their manual incompetence, of the fact that they could not change a tire or even drive a car. For me, the urge to build with my hands was once again becoming overwhelming, and renovating houses every summer was no longer enough to satisfy it.

Then came the sparkling moment with Sue Vaughn and the table in the backyard in 1971. Not long after that, I said to Mary, "I am going to quit teaching. I am going to make things out of wood." She fully agreed.

We made a plan. In place of a sabbatical, I would ask for a one-year leave of absence from my teaching position. We would see if, during that year, working together, we could make something approximating a middle-class living by crafting wooden furniture. We had no business plan, no identified market, and no particular reason to think we could succeed, but we had several things on our side. First, Mary and I share an important trait: a willingness to be poor in order to pursue a dream. One summer, when funds got low while I was in graduate school, we had two kids and literally nothing to eat but the field corn that farmers let us pick. That kind of thing breaks or strengthens a marriage. It had strengthened ours. Second, we had four healthy, strapping sons, ages six to thirteen, who could help us in the work. Third, our renovated homes had all sold quickly, persuading me that I had an eye for aesthetic decision making. And finally, we had the good fortune to have inherited our parents' work ethic. We were not only willing to sand woodwork for twelve hours straight, we actually enjoyed it. My leave began at the end of 1972, and I never went back.

Paul Guilmette, a friend and partner in our house-renovating enterprise, asked me one evening what I was going to name the new company. I offered The Dovetail Shop, New Gloucester Joiners, Shaker Inspired, and others as sound possibilities. He shook his head at each suggestion. "You should call it Thomas Moser, Furniture

Opposite: Where it all started, the Grange Hall, New Gloucester, Maine, 1972.

Maker," he said. His suggestion made sense. If a piece of furniture from a company named after me fell apart, the customer would know whom to hunt down and blame. Conversely, if, as I hoped, the furniture was good, the customer would know who was responsible, and would trust me to make more furniture for him or her. By using the eighteenth-century abbreviation "Thos." and the traditional term "Cabinet Maker" set in Antique Roman typeface, we arrived at our name. Four years later, we adopted the plural "Cabinetmakers" to reflect that we were a community.

We bought the old grange hall in New Gloucester with a borrowed eight thousand dollars. Every town in Maine had one of these halls; they were important social institutions around the turn of the last century, but this one, like many, had been abandoned sometime in the late 1950s. The local orchardist stored his apple boxes in it during the winter; it had no windows, no plumbing, and no furnace. By spring 1972, we had rehabbed it and were ready to go.

But "ready," I emphasize, is a relative term. I was clearly firing before aiming once again. My whole kit of tools was a ten-inch Craftsman table saw, a four-by-twenty-one-inch belt sander, a saber saw, and a few hand tools. A semi-serious hobbyist in those days had more and better equipment. But I was also equipped with a lifetime of pent-up enthusiasm, so I waded in. My first project was kitchen cabinets for a little house we were fixing up for resale.

Like most things we made then, these were pine. Since we had no money for materials, nearly everything we built came from boards cut from our own trees on our fifty-two-acre woodlot in New Gloucester.

Thos. Moser

Cabinet Maker

HANDCRAFTED FURNITURE

The unadorned unity and simplicity of Shaker design provide an inspiring medium for both the craftsman and client. It is our purpose and joy to use construction techniques of the 18th and 19th Centuries to create fine furniture suited to contemporary homes as well as traditional settings. Shaker designs are honest statements of functionalism.

All furniture items within our collection — and those that are custom-ordered are signed, numbered and registered to the owner.

We welcome visitors to our showroom — a restored 1760 cottage. 9 to 5 — Tuesday through Saturday.

Portfolio available upon request for $1.25.

Cobb's Bridge Road, New Gloucester, Maine 04260   207-926-4446

33

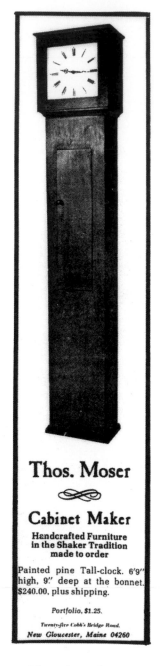

We had the logs sawn at a local sawmill, and then we air-dried them according to the ancient woodworking prescription: one year per inch of thickness.

I flirted with the concept of using only hand tools, but quickly abandoned that notion. The moment you turn on an electric light to do woodworking, you are compromising yourself. To this day, I get into disputes with purists who contend that it is dishonest to use this or that piece of power equipment for this or that operation. There is some validity to their concern. Which operations to automate and which we should preserve for handwork is a conundrum with which we still wrestle. But anyone who toured our shop then, or now, would see that skilled manual labor is still a large part of our operation. Power tools were and are adjuncts to craftsmanship, not the other way around, and I offer no apologies for labor-saving choices we have made.

The first piece of furniture I built in that old grange hall was a Shaker round stand made of walnut. My son Matthew still has it. Then, we took a commission to build a cupboard for a neighbor's kitchen. Word of mouth took over. We got another commission, then another.

I hired my first nonstudent employee, Ed Boyker, in 1974. Ed was fifty-three years old, an accomplished finish carpenter of the old school who had spent most of a lifetime building interiors for wealthy, demanding mill owners in the area. Ed was self-taught and could build anything from wood.

When I say I learned woodworking from long-dead craftsmen, that is only part of the story. I have also acquired a tremendous amount of

Left: An early ad for a tall case clock. Not only has our type-face changed, so have our prices.
Opposite: Mary in her attic office, early 1970s.

knowledge from Ed and other skilled woodworkers with whom I have worked through the years. For example, it fascinated me that Ed did virtually no measuring, working instead exclusively with "story poles," scraps of wood on which he marked crucial dimensions to determine spacings. He could build a complex and precise piece of furniture while having almost no idea of any of its dimensions in inches or feet. Today, I do much the same; it is common for me to design and build a piece with little notion of its measurements.

The learning curve was steep; lessons arrived, bidden and unbidden, every day. On one occasion, a local retired teacher, Katherine Stimets, commissioned a desk. She could pay $350. I made an oak desk for her in just five days. I had to build it quickly or I would lose money on the project. I whipped it out, a complex piece with hand-cut dovetails, eight drawers, thumbnail molding, and a double pedestal with a modesty panel in front. I took it to her house, and she gave me the money.

The next day she called. She was disappointed with how badly made it was, so I returned to her home. She was right. You could see daylight through the gap between the top and the pedestals. One drawer was too

loose, another was too tight. The desk was crude. I said to her, "But you could pay only $350. I couldn't devote any more time to it for that price. Had you given me $1,200, I could have made you a perfect desk."

"I am disappointed," she responded.

"Well, so am I," I said. "Let me make you another desk."

This time, I built a writing table, with tapered legs and a single, slim pencil drawer. It was exquisite, very delicate and feminine, well proportioned, perfectly crafted. She loved it. It was a lesson learned. It is better to do less well than more badly. That philosophy has informed our work ever since. (I never sold the eight-drawer desk. I used it in our shop to hold paint cans. It proved far more effective as an object lesson than as a piece of furniture.)

That summer, along with Ed Boyker, we hired a couple of students from Bates College. The showroom was the dining room of our house, the big 1782 center-hall Georgian just down the road from the shop. It was constructed by Col. Isaac Parsons, and we had lovingly and painstakingly restored it. Mary showed the furniture to customers and handled the advertising, accounting, and other administrative tasks. Every afternoon, our four boys got off the school bus at the shop and pitched in, doing everything from running the lathe to stacking lumber to sweeping up.

For the first three years, our "line" consisted of reproductions of American furniture that I admired. Mostly, they were pieces we copied from Sturbridge Village in Massachusetts, along with some from

We are pleased to provide you with a source of fine craftsmanship in furniture. Through the combined efforts of craftsman and client furniture is created that is unobtainable in today's market. By way of illustration recent pieces have included: A Table to seat 16 people, a Handkerchief table for a special corner, a painted dower chest for a recent graduate. Come and see us or write. We are located at 25 Cobbs Bridge Road, New Gloucester, Me., 04260.

Portfolio of ideas available for $1.25.

Thos. Moser
Cabinet Maker

"In those days, we were quite opportunistic; when the new-furniture work slacked off, we would restore old pieces, renovate houses, and even do landscaping, anything to make the payroll every Thursday."

colonial Williamsburg and the odd Shaker piece. It was case work and tables, as we weren't ready for the complex, curved geometry of chairs. The work was not quite slavish reproduction—I could not help but make the odd modification here and there—but it was close. In those days, we were quite opportunistic; when the new-furniture work slacked off, we would restore old pieces, renovate houses, and even do landscaping, anything to make the payroll every Thursday. It was often touch and go, and at times we resorted to fancy credit-card juggling, but in thirty years, we have never missed a payroll.

In 1977, I wrote a book called *How to Make Shaker Furniture*. Living in New Gloucester, Mary and I had become friendly with the small remaining Shaker community in the area. One day, I asked Sister Mildred, the eldress, what she thought of the book. She considered the question for a long time, and finally responded, "I liked it. Imitation is the sincerest form of flattery."

That statement was a punishing blow. A subconscious worry suddenly surfaced: I realized that what we had produced for three years was largely imitative, and that did not bode well. To whose equity were we contributing? Many of the designs we were building had been created by men who had been dead since 1770; we were enhancing their stature, not our own. All we were selling—our only assets—were workmanship, sharp tools, and quick hands. Then and there, I determined that we needed to create our own definitive style.

This was risky. There is always an easy, ready market for good reproductions. By definition, however, no guaranteed market existed for Thos. Moser style; indeed, at that point, I didn't even know if we had a style. On the other hand, margins for reproduction work were slim, and we lost money in each of our first three years. In fact, in 1975, we sold our house to pay off debts and underwrite the business. Since that lovely old house was right down the road from the shop, its loss served as a constant reminder that we needed to make changes.

Opposite: An eighteen-inch surface planer, still in use in the shop on Dingley Island.

But the creation of what has become our style had more than an
economic impetus. I also had a strong sense that the best design is simple,
unadorned, and in harmony with the material, and I very much wanted
to build on traditional furniture forms with those values in mind. Later
in this book, I will explore the roots of the Moser aesthetic as it
developed through the years. What I will say now, however, is that
it worked. People liked it.

The business grew. We bought a church vestry in New Gloucester,
chainsawed it into four sections, hauled them on a flatbed trailer, and
reassembled them next to the grange hall; the vestry became our
showroom. Slowly, we got out of the business of house restoration and
antiques repair and concentrated on building new furniture.

We began to draw a profile of the average Thos. Moser Cabinetmakers
customer. He or she was generally well educated and fairly affluent, but
affluence was far from the most important criterion. We came to realize
that a green Volvo pulling into the lot meant a sure sale, while a Cadillac
was more iffy. In short, our customers seemed to be much like us, people

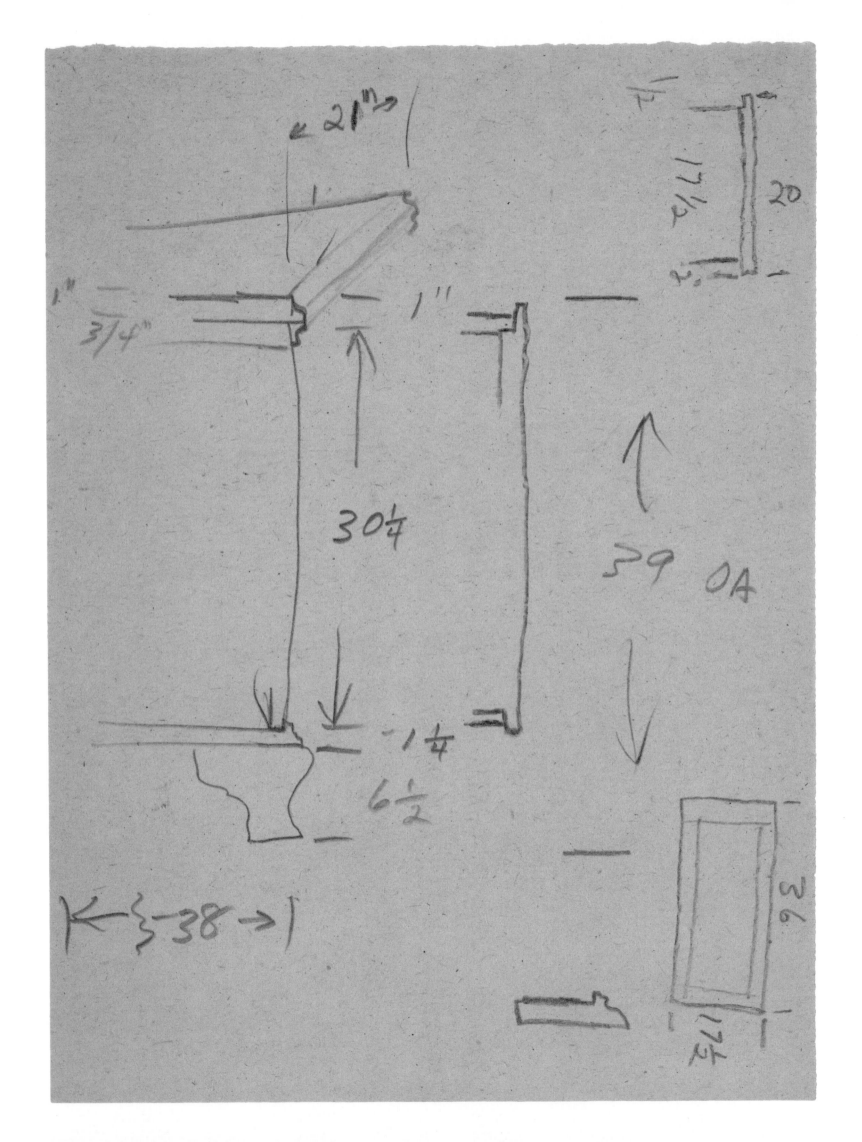

Moving the Vestry

Many liberal religions in rural Maine suffered from shrinking membership throughout the twentieth century. This led to a wealth of abandoned churches dotting the countryside, most in poor repair, and most available for purchase for little or—if the buyer was willing to move it—nothing. In 1974, for the token sum of five dollars, I was able to secure an 1839 church and vestry building from the Northeast District Universalist Church. I turned the church building and grounds over to the New Gloucester Historical Society, which agreed to take responsibility for the church if I

removed the abandoned vestry building. Around the same time, a one-acre lot next to our grange-hall workshop became available, and we bought it.

This was our chance to create a showroom for Mary. We planned to move the old vestry to the lot and use it to store, display, and sell furniture. This would free up the 1762 gambrel house that we had been using for the purpose, and we could then restore and eventually occupy the house as our family home.

I hired David Carney, a weightlifter and rough carpenter, to take off the vestry's roof and cut the remaining post-and-beam

building into four equal parts. By running a chain saw lengthwise down the center of the seven-by-seven-inch timbers, he had the job done in three days. Although the roof sheathing was rotten, we saved all the timbers. The building was now ready to move in four parts on an equipment trailer owned by an excavation contractor, Fred Hunnewell.

We managed to jack up, load, haul, remove, and position the first three sections without incident. But the fourth one was trouble. With a two-holer privy room protruding from it, it was too wide to fit through the planked sides of the old

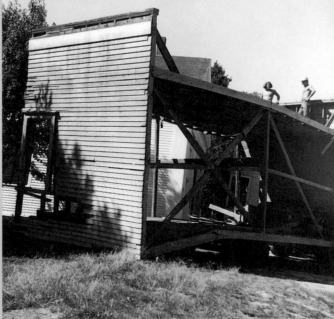

wooden railroad bridge that spans the tracks of the Grand Trunk. Fred drove the section onto the bridge, but it got stuck halfway across.

"What should I do?" he yelled.

"Put her in low gear and go! We can't just leave it here!" I shouted back. Go he did, and no fewer that six sideboards and some small portion of the outhouse tore loose and tumbled to the tracks thirty feet below.

We nailed the boards back to the bridge, but not before Keith Littlefield, our resident state policeman, came by and asked for our permit.

"Permit? What permit?" Since we were nearly done, he shrugged, cautioned us about low-hanging wires, and drove off into the twilight.

We bolted the four sections together in the center of the lot. Once in place, we completed the foundation and the roof. Mary now had her showroom with a wood stove for heat and the two-holer for storing catalogs and supplies.

who preferred an artful melding of form and function over something designed solely around surface appeal.

While people would drive some distance to seek us out in New Gloucester, this little town of eight hundred was something short of the crossroads of the Western world. Our first expansion, in 1976, was to lease a showroom in the Old Port section of downtown Portland. After two fairly successful years there, we closed it down and moved back to New Gloucester because the two sites, only thirty miles apart, served the same market. When our line grew, in 1984, we bought an abandoned brick building on Cumberland and Forest Avenues in Portland, a lovely place with ten thousand square feet of airy, high-ceilinged space. We did a complete restoration, and sold furniture there for the next fourteen years.

On the production end, we outgrew the New Gloucester shop, and in 1980 we bought a former meatpacking plant on Riverside Drive in Auburn, Maine. We rehabbed the building and made good use of the twenty-one-thousand square feet.

By now we had thirty employees, and it was an interesting collection of personalities, including a former attorney, a Ph.D. oceanographer from M.I.T., several women who were exploring alternative lifestyles, and a number of college-educated apprentices who used us as a stepping-stone to establishing their own one-man shops. These people found themselves elbow to elbow with working-class people from Maine mill towns like Lewiston, Jay, and Lisbon Falls, and the interaction was fascinating. The academic refugees tended to get high-minded about art and integrity; their mill-town counterparts served as a reality check for them. The academics felt, and some still feel, that there should be a disconnect between doing

craft and making a living; that the work is pure only if it bankrupts you. My view—and the view of many of the second- and third-generation mill workers, with whom my sympathies typically lie—is that craftsmanship should be seen in the nineteenth-century sense. In those days, a journeyman developed unique skills and produced things of value and longevity, and consequently had every right to make a living at it.

By the mid-eighties, even the Riverside shop was not big enough, and we laid plans to consolidate the two shops into a single, one-floor plant. Using the factory model we had found on trips to Denmark and Sweden, in 1987 we built the efficient, comfortable sixty-five-thousand-square-foot shop we use today.

One by one, our sons returned to the business. Upon graduation from high school, each had set his own course. Matthew moved to Boston and later Portland to pursue antique restoration; Andrew joined the Air Force; Aaron graduated from the Culinary Institute of America and worked as an executive chef in Dallas; and David, our youngest, graduated from the University of Maine and did a tour with the Peace Corps in Kenya. All but Matthew still work with us today: Andrew is a craftsman who helped design and build the Auburn shop, Aaron manages all of our corporate and institutional selling efforts, and David runs the prototype shop, producing new designs and one-of-a-kind

Failures

By any measure, we have been successful. We have created a company that has flourished for thirty years. While our growth has generally consisted of one small success breeding another, larger one, the process has been far from seamless. Our efforts were, and are, punctuated by plenty of failures.

One failure in particular stands out. When we moved into the new shop in 1987, I had to find a use for the old, now-empty shop. I love late-Victorian wooden toys. They are beautiful and seem so permanent, and are far superior to the plastic molded stuff found on many store shelves today. This affinity, perhaps augmented by the fact that I had just become a grandfather for the first time, prompted me to fill

that empty shop with an enterprise that manufactured wooden toys. We hired three people, bought and installed machinery, created an office, built a dozen prototypes, and dreamed up a name: Companion Manufacturing Company. Our motto was, Things Made Better Than They Need to Be.

We proceeded to craft a series of miniature strollers, toy boxes, wagons, sleds, child-sized chairs and tables, and more. The operation was a wonderful sight to see, almost like Santa's workshop, and we had fun.

Our bubble burst in about six months. Fine craftsmanship and quality materials are never cheap. Our toys were so expensive that, while plenty of people admired them, almost nobody bought them. Stuck with a

mountain of unsold inventory, we closed the doors. For almost two years, I didn't have to pay income tax because of the massive write-off.

Through the years, there were many other failures: ill-fated stabs at making daycare furniture and "affordable" chairs, mass mailings to the wrong people, showrooms in the wrong places, buying a truckload of poor-quality local cherry in a noble attempt to support Maine commerce, and purchasing tons of old cast-iron machinery at auction because it was beautiful rather than necessary. None, however, was as ill-advised as that wonderful, ridiculous company that made perfect, too-expensive-for-play toys.

Left: An adjustable music chair and stand built as a commission. Neither was successful as an off-the-shelf offering.
Above: Products of the short-lived Companion Manufacturing Company.

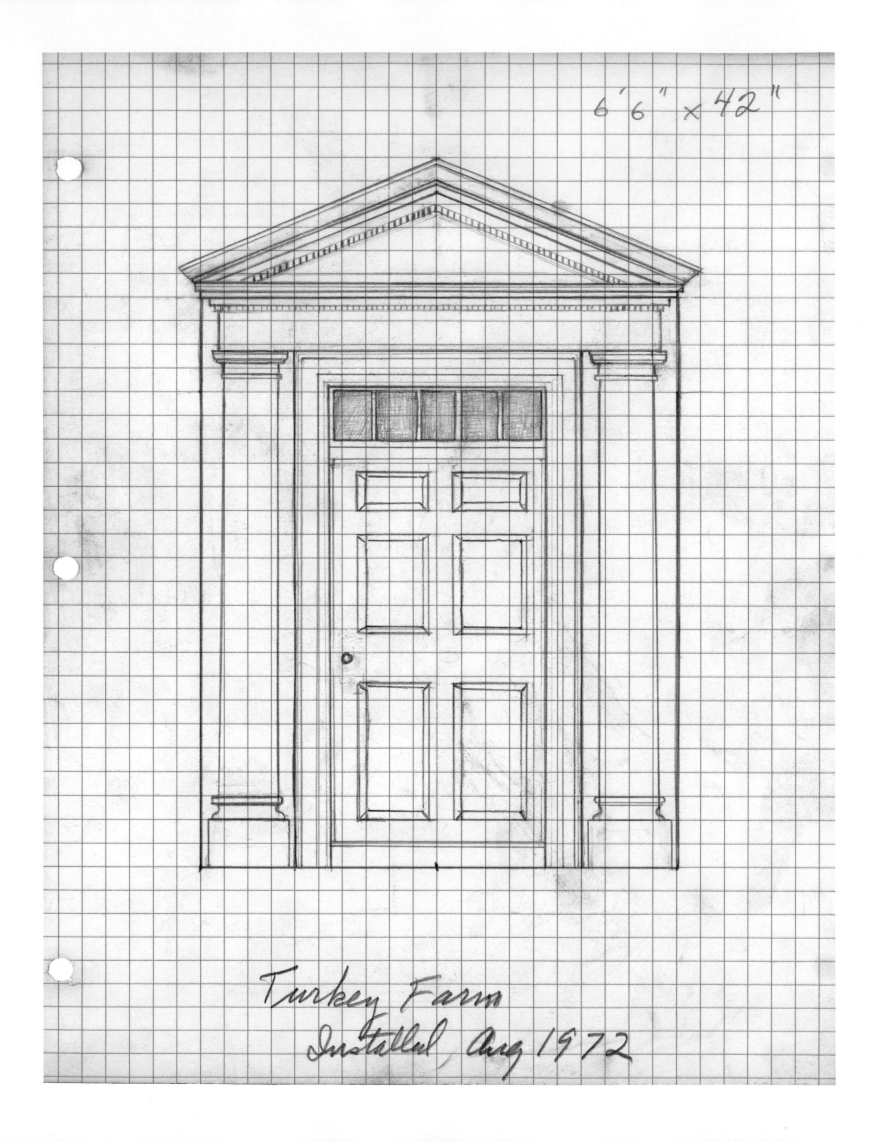

6'6" × 42"

Turkey Farm
Installed Aug 1972

commissioned pieces. Their skills are invaluable. Without them, I doubt we would still be in business.

In August 1995, I hired Harry Fraser, a seasoned executive, to serve as CEO. He has proved a great blessing, since making astute financial decisions was never my long suit.

After many years of shepherding this enterprise, I feel that it has a life and inertia of its own. I am not only persuaded that Thos. Moser Cabinetmakers will survive me, but I am also amazed to realize that, at last count, twenty-three employees have left the company and

Opposite: In the early days, we did custom woodwork of all kinds, including this new front entrance for a two-hundred-year-old house.
Right: Our son Andrew was a great helper in the old Grange Hall. Mostly he was the janitor; today, he is a skilled craftsman, proficient in all aspects of furniture construction.

"I am not only persuaded that Thos. Moser Cabinetmakers will survive me, but I am also amazed to realize that, at last count, twenty-three employees have left the company and started furniture-building businesses of their own."

started furniture-building businesses of their own. While I view this development with mixed emotion—no employer likes to train people only to have them become competitors—on the whole, I am pleased that I've been able to persuade twenty-three people of a truth that few believed when I started in 1972: making quality furniture out of wood is an economically viable career choice.

In 1994, Mary and I built a house on a rocky point on Dingley Island. Accessible by bridge, it is about a forty-minute drive from our Auburn shop. The idea was that I would relax here, but it is not working out that way. I find that detaching myself from Thos. Moser Cabinetmakers is more difficult than I had imagined. I still go to work three or four days a week and actively develop new products for manufacture, although I retain no operational responsibilities.

With this book, I hope to convey the thinking behind the aesthetic and structural design choices I have made. I hope that woodworkers, artists, architects, designers, and those who simply like our furniture will learn something from my long and sometimes painful experience, as I have learned so much from others through the years.

But perhaps more than that, I want to give some sense of the passion that keeps me, at age sixty-seven, still engaged in designing and building things out of wood. The joy of teaching the craft to others and observing their growth remains strong. The thrill that I felt that day in the backyard of my home thirty years ago is still very much with me. I am convinced that it will live as long as I live.

Opposite: Looking south from the porch at the Dingley Island barn. The view is ever changing with the season, the time of day, the wind direction, the weather—even the mood of the viewer.

Chapter 2
A COVENANT WITH WOOD

Opposite: Detail of a dove-tailed drawer.
Above: The ash legs of the cherry Crescent Stool are wedged from the top, guaranteeing a long and useful life.

With rare exceptions, the furniture we produce is made of American black cherry. My emotional bond with this wood runs deep. A piece of furniture—in fact, any created object—is a unique confluence of design, workmanship, and material, and each element bears responsibility for the success or failure of the whole. When people admire our furniture, they tend to rhapsodize about the first two elements. In contrast, I consider the material to be the essential feature.

I have admired cherry since I first saw it forty years ago, when a few of the antique tables and chairs we bought and repaired in upstate New York were made of this extraordinary wood. But I did not build new furniture from it. In the early seventies, when we were starting out, we primarily used native species cut from our own woodlot in New Gloucester: beech, maple, birch, oak, and ash. Employing these, known in the woodworking trade as "select northern hardwoods," made sense for two reasons: they were the same species that the early New England craftsmen, whose furniture we were reproducing, had used, and cutting and curing our own boards kept our operating expenses low in those lean early years. Twice a year, local logger Howard Ripley and I would cruise the woodlot and take down only the mature trees.

Then, the sawyer in New Gloucester sawed the logs into boards for us. We air-dried them either behind the house or at the grange-hall shop.

In those days, we would also tear down old houses and barns to salvage material, a practice I greatly enjoyed as it spared living trees and resulted in pieces with instant historic gravitas. In the early seventies, two-hundred-year-old architecture was often seen as useless surplus, and carried little value among the Mainers who were born in this cultural heritage. They saw old Cape Cod and colonial timber-framed houses as drafty and antiquated, devoid of aesthetic or economic

value. In a five-year period, we salvaged material from at least six houses and two barns, all from the eighteenth or early nineteenth century, at the request of owners who them saw only as liabilities. Imagine the inventory of pumpkin-pine flooring, Christian doors, and raised paneling this yielded. Often the wood retained the original finish of buttermilk-and-iron-oxide red paint, which we incorporated into its reuse as furniture. We built many reproduction pieces from this reclaimed old-growth material, including several case pieces that no doubt initially confused the discriminating eye of more than one antiques dealer (we signed all pieces to avoid misrepresentation).

Despite my admiration for American black cherry, we used very little in the early days because the species, *Prunus serotina*, is not native to Maine. In fact, the only species of the *Prunus* genus that grows wild here is pin cherry, *Prunus pensylvanica*, a prolific "weed" tree that typically reaches only a few inches in diameter, overgrows stone walls and hedgerows, and is the favorite food of tent caterpillars.

But when, in 1976, we made a conscious decision to create our own style, we began using black cherry—and ash for spindle members— almost exclusively, and have ever since. This is inconvenient and expensive, as every cherry board must be trucked over five hundred miles from Pennsylvania, but we have never regretted the choice.

Left: Logs are scaled for size. Using a measuring stick that computes diameter and length, each log is marked with the number of board feet it will yield. A board foot is a cubic unit measuring twelve inches by twelve inches, one inch thick.
Opposite: American black cherry, Allegheny Plateau, Pennsylvania. Courtesy Kane Hardwood.

Why cherry? First and foremost, it is beautiful. Cherry has color, but that term is too simple to describe the appeal of sunlight and shadow on a sanded, oiled, waxed board. The wood has a unique translucence, evoking a reflecting pool rather than a simple mirror. The auburn hues reside not only on the surface, but also inside, and they are visible as such. In my view, no wood can rival the depth and complexity of cherry's color and figure, although mahogany and walnut come close.

I have found that, more than any other wood, cherry, when finished with rubbed oil and wax, invites people to touch it. Many customers say our furniture has as much tactile as visual appeal, and that they cannot pass a piece without running a hand across it. Perhaps this is due to some atavistic desire to be warmed by the campfire; when face-sawn, the grain evokes dancing flames and radiates the impression of trapped heat. Whatever the reason, after more than three decades of intimate

Opposite: Keeping track of wood grain direction and color. Often, when a piece fails aesthetically, it is because this step was done too quickly.
Right: The ambitious corner of a wooden sofa.
Following pages: The Continuous Arm Bench. The arm is a lamination formed from ten thin strips, all from the same piece of wood.

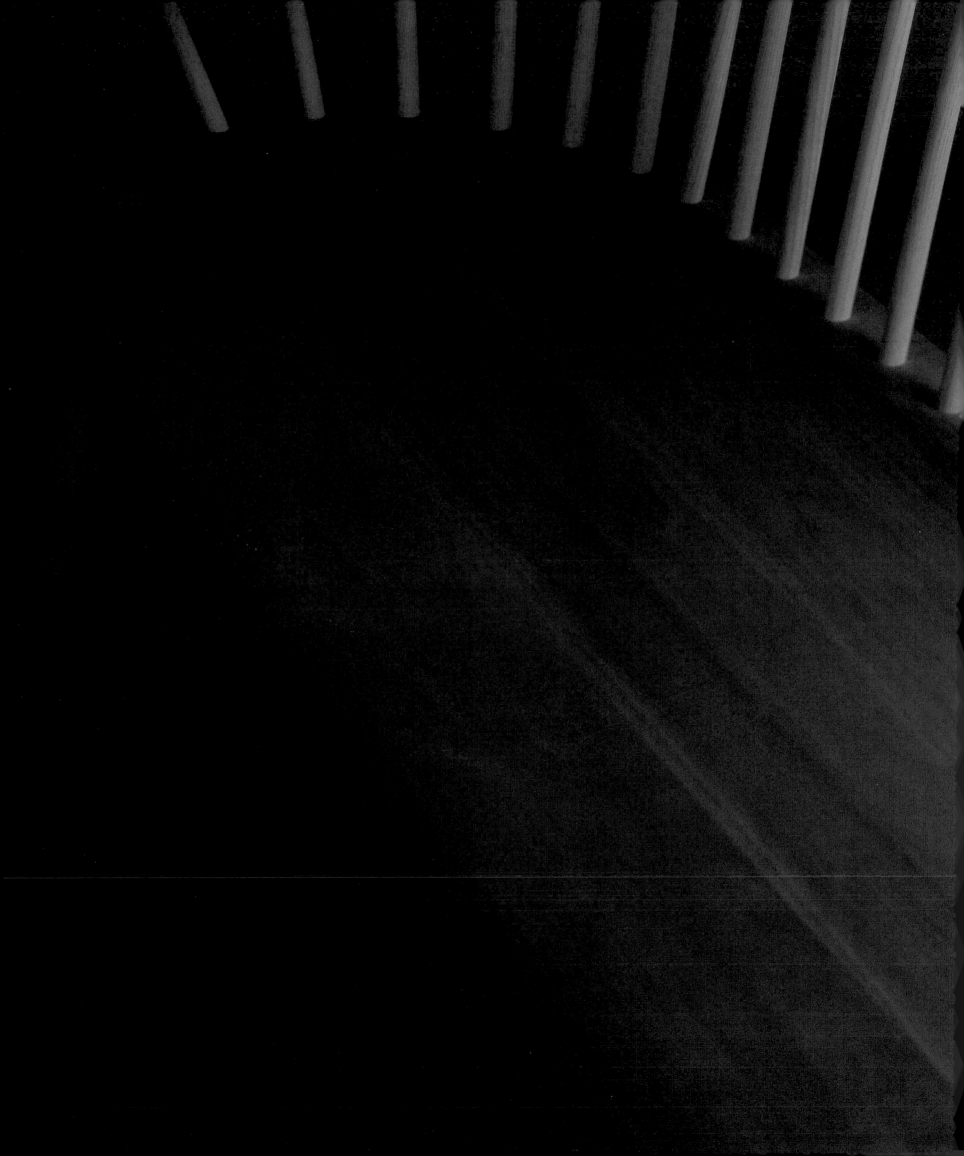

Left: As cherry is exposed to sunlight and air it changes color, shifting from a light salmon to a deep, rich reddish-brown. The sample at the bottom is three months old.
Opposite: Chair seat detail. The wedge locks the leg into the seat. Making the joinery visible assures the sitter of the chair's integrity.
Following pages: (on left) Detail of sculpted stool. (on right) Select-grade three-inch lumber for the top rail of a sleigh bed. Numbers indicate a set for headboard and foot-board. These thick boards are so beautiful, I often hate to cut them.

association with this wood, I still feel the pull. I can't pass without a touch, either.

When freshly cut or sanded, cherry is tannish pink, pale, and not particularly lovely. But the wood is rich in resins, particularly prussic acid, that react rapidly to both light and oxygen, so cherry achieves in six months the patina that oak or maple acquires only after six decades. A bedrock tenet of my aesthetic judgment is that beauty is inseparable from integrity; that things are beautiful almost precisely to the degree that they celebrate their true nature, so I am always loathe to stain, bleach, fume, paint, or otherwise artificially color any wood. That conviction narrowed my wood palette considerably, as walnut, butternut, and cherry are the only American hardwoods with intrinsic color to any degree. Walnut is too dark and formal for most tastes, and butternut is too soft for the demands of fine furniture, and too rare. Cherry's color comfortably straddles the formal/informal divide, and while the stock is dwindling, there are enough trees if they are harvested and used wisely.

Cherry is also highly workable. With any species of wood, the denser the cell growth, the easier it is to machine, and the better it holds

its shape afterward. In this sense, rock maple is perhaps the ultimate; it holds sharp, clean edges. But cherry machines extraordinarily well, as long as one approaches it respectfully. Due to the high concentration of volatile tannins, it burns easily, so woodworkers must use sharp tools, and keep the stock, or the tool, constantly moving. With other woods —ash comes to mind—one can "cheat" in the sanding process, going from coarse 80-grit paper to the final 220-grit sanding and achieve a perfect polish. Cherry suffers no such shortcuts. One must dutifully progress from 80 to 120 to 180 to 220 to 400 grit; if not, the material will require such vigorous and prolonged sanding to remove scratch marks that it will burn, or at least discolor. Cherry is also difficult to steam bend; overheating turns it a singed purple.

But these are not insurmountable difficulties. We keep our tools sharp, we sand carefully, and we are highly selective in outsourcing our steam bending. For most curved elements, particularly structural ones, we use a multi-ply lamination to achieve great strength, although we steam bend chair-crest rails and ladderback slats with good results.

Cherry is stable; once dried, it is even less prone to seasonal movement than is black walnut, which many believe is the most stable American hardwood. This stability allows us to make relatively large panels, which is a big plus with our furniture, as we panel the backs of our case pieces to make them as presentable as the fronts. If case work is built in solid wood, the surfaces must be broken up with stiles, rails, and floating panels, not simply for aesthetic purposes, but to anticipate and compensate for the inevitable seasonal movement the wood will experience. Cherry has an expansion coefficient of ninety-two to one, which means for each unit of measure it swells in length during summer humidity, it swells ninety-two units in width. Expressed another way, cherry, like most woods, does not swell in length, but it does in width, hence frame-and-panel construction. But that amount of swelling is modest compared to that of other woods, so the panels can be more than twice as large as those in, say, English oak.

Cherry takes a nonmembrane finish well, adapting more easily than some of the oil-rich hardwoods such as teak or open-grained oaks. The use of any finish must always spring from respect for the material.

Opposite: A back detail of a frame-and-panel case. This is the same engineering used in building a post-and-beam barn.

The Province of Maine Collection

Early in our history, we worked mostly in pine and other local woods, much as the Shakers had done a century before. To protect their work, the Shakers, along with most Maine house carpenters of the time, painted exposed surfaces with natural tints such as iron oxide, indigo blue, lamp black, and burnt umber, mixed usually with a base of buttermilk and occasionally with a blend of white lead and linseed oil. We came to know the colors well from furniture fragments and antique houses, and we spent a good deal of time replicating them, first in buttermilk and later in synthetic bases. We applied these homemade formulations to our furniture, and then we used wax to give the matte finish a little sheen and protection from water. The result was good, and in many cases our finish looked much the same as that of the antiques.

While the Williamsburg and Sturbridge Village companies offered paint in period colors, none matched those we had found in early Maine pieces. We commissioned an Auburn company, Maine Line Paints, to mix an array of acrylic-based paints for us. Soon, customers began showing as much interest in the paint as the furniture, so we created the Province of Maine paint collection, which we sold in our showrooms along with our furniture.

We discontinued the line in the late 1970s, after we made the transition to oiled-and-waxed cherry, but those colors and their evocative names—many taken from families or landmarks in New Gloucester— live on in my memory: Gambrel Brown, Opportunity, Intervale, Ox Blood, Chandler Gold, Cobb's Bridge Blue, Lichen Green, Parson's Putty, and Cape Ann Blue. While we no longer sell the paint, I still have a fond place in my heart for it and for traditional painted furniture. Even today, the only large piece in my office is an early Dr. White's chest, resplendent in Ox Blood– coated pine.

The same colors as were used by the early settlers of Maine…

Essentially two paint bases were used during the Colonial period—sour buttermilk and white lead in linseed oil. The lead is poisonous and the odor of sour buttermilk is awful. To color the bases, people added natural substances; among them were carbon, animal blood, berry juice, various oxides and clay.

These homemade paints were subject to chalking and chipping, so for interior durability they often rubbed on beeswax. The running and fading of paint on exteriors was a problem never solved in colonial times as you can see by examining the powder stained foundations of the vintage homes.

Antique homes still displaying their authentic colors are not uncommon in Maine, in places like New Gloucester, Castine and Wiscasset. These colors existed two hundred years ago and work beautifully today on the furniture and homes of the Colonial and Post Revolutionary periods.

The Province of Maine Collection is the product of practical experience in restoring old houses and furniture. It is the result of match testing, not only in our lab, but against the original furniture and houses themselves. We use a safer water-latex base—the best possible acrylic—and many of the same natural pigments as the settlers used. The result is a museum-quality reproduction of these authentic colors.

Gambrel Brown

An outstanding exterior color which changes with the sun, Gambrel Brown is particularly suited to a wooded setting where your dwelling will blend with and not contest your environment.

Opportunity

This strong earth tone comes from clay pigments that may have been mined in south-eastern Androscoggin County, Maine. It comprises yellow, gold and mustard. It is commonly found on interior trim as well as full exteriors.

Intervale

Intervale takes its name from a tree-shaded section of New Gloucester, Maine. Like Chandler Gold, this color derives from marine clay and hints green and yellow leaf tones. It works splendidly in connecting red to brown, and green to brown rooms, as well as papered to unpapered walls. As in all putties it was used also as an exterior color.

Ox Blood

The early New Englander mixed animal blood, iron oxide and sour buttermilk with lampblack or chimney soot to achieve this deep red shade. It is found on exteriors, outbuildings, interior woodwork and a great variety of country furniture. Adding a light coat of tinted paste wax gives a warm, earthy luster.

Chandler Gold

Our Maine ancestors were partial to the richness of Chandler Gold, a color with an affinity to grey and brown. It is right both indoors and outdoors, for whole rooms, especially living rooms, and a congenial unassertive overall covering for the exterior.

Cobb's Bridge Blue

Blueberries and elderberries were crushed and mixed with indigo to make this paint. Dark blue was used particularly on interior objects and is a very difficult color to replicate. It offers a highly satisfying contrast against white plaster walls.

Lichen Green

This green, so popular with early Americans, came from copper oxide most of which had to be purchased. To this they added earthen yellows and lampblack for a hard wearing yet dignified color. There were several general uses for this green; exterior trim, certain case furniture, and most interestingly, floors. A covering of varnish, when applied to floors offers excellent durability as well as a depth and translucence.

Parson's Putty

A universal putty, this is darker, cooler and greener than Intervale and was discovered in several Antique house restorations. With tinted waxing, a hall, staircase or balustrade are impressive in this color. As a background for pictures, a transitional color or a trim; Parsons Putty will fit in well. This is an interesting exterior color in a wooded setting.

Cape Ann Blue

The settlers from Cape Ann, Massachusetts moved to New Gloucester, Maine in the mid 18th century. They brought with them an interest in classical art and architecture. This light blue is the color closely associated with the Adams Brothers and with Wedgewood in England. It was the foundation color for Hepplewhite and Sheridan designs and is a magnificent color for early 19th century restorations.

Maine Line Paints
Gagnon-Haskell, Inc., 13 Hutchins St. Auburn, Maine 04210

Left: We created the original Province of Maine brochure with actual paint splotches for color samples.
Opposite: A page from Tom's sketchbook shows the plan for the inverted arm chair.

SET TAPER at 1"

1"

Inverted Arm Bench

— figure 1 —

$2\frac{1}{8}$ 5" $7\frac{1}{4}$

25

43¾ 45 47⅞ 49 48

blank outline

seat dimensions

4"

$6\frac{1}{2}$"

leg holes

$13\frac{3}{4}$

1" $1\frac{1}{8}$"

4"

ctr.

3⅞

3¾

$3\frac{1}{2}$"

arm mortise ¾" diameter

— front —

Choose blank, mark center line then outer dimensions.
Locate arm mortise and leg hole sites, leg holes are 1" diameter, arm mortise
is ¾".

Use settee drilling guides to drill back leg holes. Use guide marked
with cute little cherries ∞" to drill front leg holes. Use the jig labelled appropriately
to drill arm mortise.

Trace seat outline and hilite using appropriate patterns. Hilite pattern
is also used to mark spindle hole sites 1-6. (see figure 2).

— figure 2 —

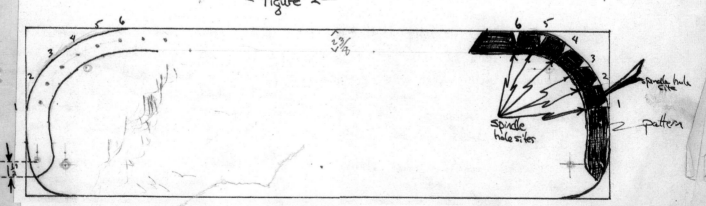

6 5 4 3 2 1

$2\frac{3}{4}$

6 5 4 3 2 1

spindle hole site

spindle hole sites

pattern

$1\frac{7}{8}$ $1\frac{13}{16}$

The hole sites between the sixes are marked with pattern (2 x 2 cherry thing).

"I discovered that oil warmed to about 130 degrees penetrated wonderfully. While a drop of room-temperature oil would slowly and reluctantly soak into wood, a heated drop vanished into it like melted butter on a cotton shirt."

Given that tenet, perhaps the most reverential finish for our work would be none at all. This is what many Scandinavian masters do with their finest pieces. On several trips to Denmark, and in discussions with Hans Wegner, a Danish national treasure and leading European chair designer, I've discovered that the Danes' best work is left unfinished. Pieces are maintained with an annual rubdown with steel wool or fine sandpaper.

But the reality of modern life and of the American market in particular requires some finish. Water on unfinished wood can irreparably stain it, so a life of Zen-like calm and order is needed to preserve the integrity of naked wood. Most people, myself included, can't muster such a life (although the white-ash trim in our shop interior remains unfinished and beautiful after thirteen years of service).

So what kind of finish shows the greatest respect for the material? Most furniture receives what I call a membrane finish, that is, a more or less impermeable film such as paint, lacquer, shellac, varnish, or polyurethane. But if the film is ever broached—if it cracks, peels, or wears away—the underlying wood can be ruined by water. Varnish and polyurethane, along with other high-tech epoxies, are subject to ultraviolet breakdown; they lose their sheen and turn milky. Cellulose lacquer, on the other hand, retains its "gin clear" transparency but breaks down from moisture and even moderate use.

Worst of all, membrane finishes cannot be repaired. When they are scratched, alligatored, or turn chalky, the only remedy is to strip away the entire finish and refinish the piece. Nonmembrane finishes, that is, oil finishes, are forgiving. A little fine sanding and a little oil applied to the area needing repair and the job is done.

Left: A Hans Wegner chair. He has done more to advance twentieth-century chair design than any other designer.
Opposite: Bill Kasaris selecting lumber for color, grain, and stability.

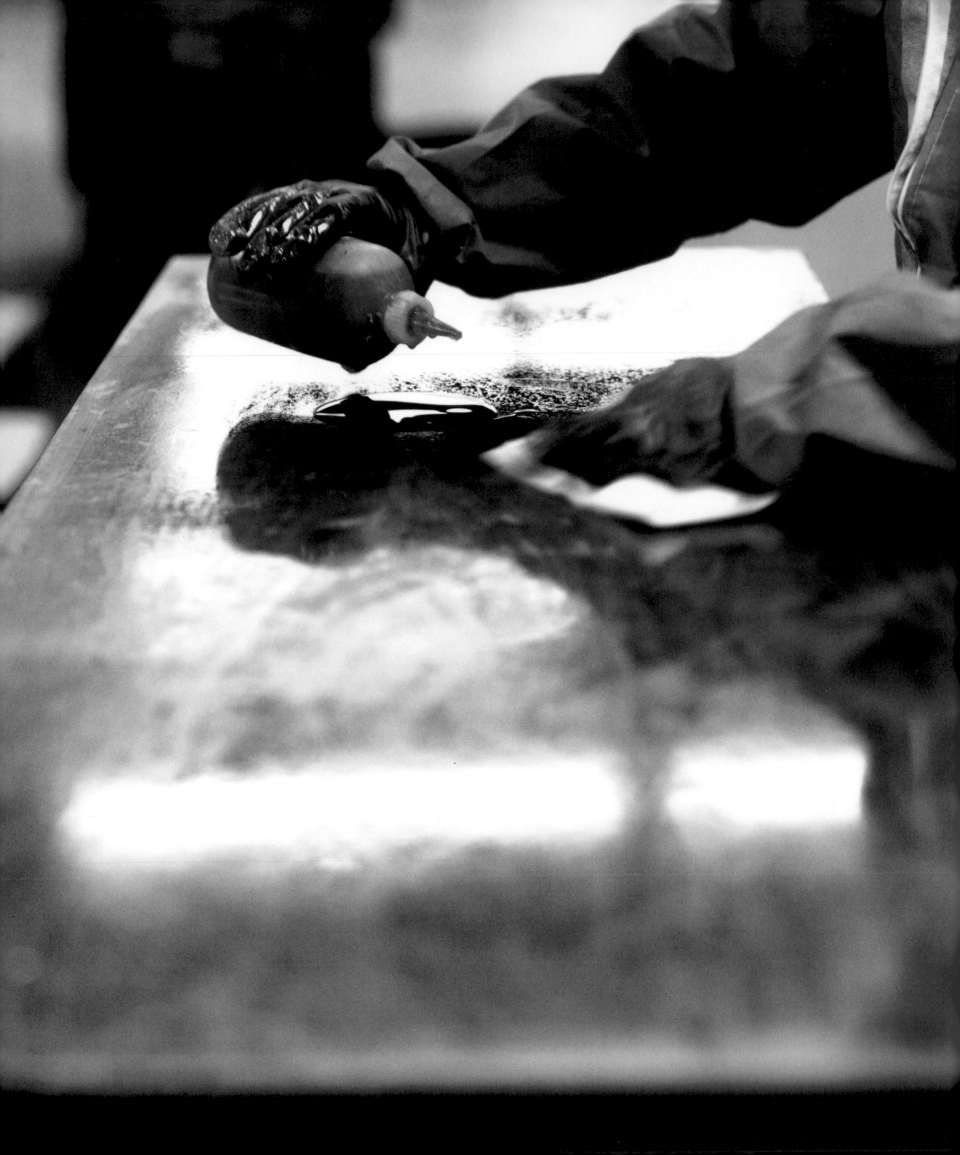

Opposite and above: Luis Reynoso applying heated linseed oil in the finishing room.

Practical considerations aside, whenever I see wood encased in a thick membrane, I have a mental image of it suffocating.

We used paint and polyurethane in response to customer desires in the early years, but I experimented from the beginning with many types of oil finishes. In 1974, I came across the time-honored method for treating a gun stock at the end of hunting season: rub it briskly with boiled linseed oil to "case harden" the surface. The hand-friction heat lowers the oil's viscosity, allowing deeper penetration. With an old walnut gun stock, a gorgeous luster and a surface tension that repels water are the result.

I realized that simple friction was not the only way to develop heat. I began warming boiled linseed oil on a hot plate, experimenting with temperatures from tepid to over 400 degrees Fahrenheit. I discovered that oil warmed to about 130 degrees penetrated wonderfully. While a drop of room-temperature oil would slowly and reluctantly soak into wood, a heated drop vanished into it like melted butter on a cotton shirt.

Finally, in 1976, we settled on the finish we use today. First, we polish the surface to a 400-grit finish. Then, using a spray gun or a soft

Opposite: Here cherry is used in the furniture and wall paneling, which complements the flooring of matched Burmese teak.
Right: We apply hot oil with compressed air.
Following pages: The Thoreau Institute library at Walden Woods. The furniture design was a collaboration between the architect and Thos. Moser Cabinetmakers. Each piece serves the special mission of the institute.

cotton rag, depending upon the size of the piece, we apply a coat of 130-degree boiled linseed oil. We allow the oil to soak in for half an hour, wipe away the excess, then wait a day and rub the whole piece with Scotchbrite, a synthetic abrasive equivalent to traditional 0000 steel wool. In the case of tabletops, we may also rub down with 400-grit wet-and-dry sandpaper. We repeat the process twice more, for a total of three coats of linseed oil applied over four or five days. Finally, we rub on two coats of Butcher's Bowling Alley wax, which is a mix of carnauba wax and beeswax, rubbing vigorously by hand in the direction of the grain.

This is an extraordinarily labor- and time-intensive finish, but the result is wonderful: the wood seems to come to life again. Polyurethane is tougher in the short term, but I have never found a more durable finish than ours in the long run. After about five years, the volatile elements of linseed oil have evaporated to leave the finish, like that on the gun stock, "case hardened." You can stand a sweaty lemonade glass on it overnight and find nary a ring the next day.

Although our furniture is made principally of cherry, we follow the traditional furniture-building practice and use northern white ash for parts that require great tensile strength, such as chair legs and spindles. The tensile strength and fabulously long, straight grain of ash make it

Above: Our sideboard shows a strong Arts and Crafts influence.
Opposite: Hot linseed oil reveals the glow inherent in well-polished cherry wood.

Evolution of the Deacon's Bench

I n no art form is the adage "History is prologue to the future" more applicable than in furniture design. One of my great pleasures is to trace design influences from generation to generation, and from one culture to another. Chairs, in particular, fascinate me. All have similar dimensions and proportions, but once the function of the chair is served, one is free to improve upon the past, and untold millions of anonymous craftsmen have been doing so for centuries.

In asserting the existence of universal truth, Plato, in one of his dialogues, speaks of "chairness," a flawless, if ethereal, form that encompasses all of the attributes of the perfect chair. With due respect to Plato, I doubt it. As someone who has spent a lifetime looking at, thinking about, sitting in, studying, designing, building, selling, and repairing chairs, I can assert the following

Clockwise from center: Shaker bench circa 1850, Deacons Bench by Thos. Moser Cabinetmakers, George Nakashima bench, New England meetinghouse bench, primitive Japanese version of Moser bench by Yoshio Tabuchi, Kawakami, Japan.

with some authority: the chair has not been built that cannot be improved upon. Yet even I seek the perfect chair, not because I think it can be found, but because I enjoy the journey.

My search for chairness always starts with the past and moves forward through history. The New England deacon's bench illustrates that trek. Every traditional American meetinghouse had its benches

88

either built into pews or as freestanding wooden planks supported by several pairs of legs. By 1830, a design evolved featuring a contoured seat, vertical spindles, and a crest at the back, all of which did a fair job of supporting the body in relative comfort during the usual three-hour sermon. These benches, usually made of pine, were long enough to support eight people and came with or without arms. In more fashionable environments, they were painted and decorated to look like rosewood or mahogany.

The Shakers developed a simplified version of these benches for their meetinghouses, making them lighter. This made the pieces easier to move to the perimeter of the room to provide space for the sect's rhythmic "shaking" dances. But I out-Shakered the Shakers years ago when I redesigned the bench once again, removing the lower stretcher altogether and pushing the piece toward an absolute minimum of ornamentation.

While I fancy that I am now approaching ultimate chairness—or, perhaps, benchness —with this design, I am persuaded by long experience that there is more, or perhaps less, to come. The chair that embodies transcendent chairness is a goal that recedes forever, and I don't believe I would have it any other way.

much better than cherry for those elements in which the wood needs to bend but not break.

For most applications, however, cherry is nearly perfect; its only flaw from our perspective is that it does not grow in commercial quantities in Maine. The cherry that we prize comes primarily from a ten-thousand-square-mile patch of the Allegheny Plateau in northwestern Pennsylvania, where the rain, temperature, and mineral content of the soil yield perfect logs. (While black cherry can be found in much of the eastern United States, the northern varieties in New York state yield greenish and brown rather than rich auburn wood, and the southern types, from West Virginia to the Mexican border, have too many black-pitch pockets.) Cherry is an opportunistic species: birds, raccoons, and other animals eat the small, black fruits, then deposit seeds in their scat in open fields. When the nation's first oil drillers denuded northwestern Pennsylvania's woodlands in the 1860s, cherry seedlings sprang up. Today, one in five timber-sized trees in the region is a cherry. A mature tree is seventy feet in height with a trunk diameter of about two feet.

Left: The dovetail joint. In the early days, we cut these by hand; today, we use a router mounted in a jig.
Opposite: Detail of Deacon's Bench, revealing the single glue line in the seat. Generally, the fewer glue lines, the better furniture looks, but it is becoming increasingly difficult to find wide cherry boards.

"Quite simply, the wood is so precious and so threatened that it is a crime to make ugly or impermanent things from it. Our furniture is crafted to last for well over a century, but frankly I believe some pieces, with care, could last five hundred years or more."

Left: The Courtroom Chair, a variation on an old theme. It looks square, but is in fact a symphony of subtle curves.
Following pages: A lounge at Pennsylvania State University at Kutztown.

American cherry has had a checkered history. While much prized by nineteenth-century cabinetmakers—it was called "poor man's mahogany"—the wood enjoyed benign neglect for much of the early twentieth century, possibly because popular tastes were running toward stained pine and oak, not to mention plastic and chrome. Indeed, the wood fell into such obscurity that a 1952 book, *Timbers of the World*, identified cherry as "formerly prized for cabinetwork and fine furniture in the United States, but its principal use now is for making blocks for electrotypes."

When I started using cherry in 1976, the wholesale cost of a board foot of FAS (Firsts and Seconds, the highest grade of wood established by the National Hardwood Lumber Association, yielding about 90 percent clear cuttings) was $1.25. But the price climbed to $3.50 by 2001 and is rising as cherry has become increasingly popular, and not just in this country. When Mary and I strolled through the International Furniture Fair in Milan, Italy, in 1996, we were amazed to see that at least one-third of the furniture on display was made of American black cherry with a faux oil finish. In the eighties, Europeans had no idea this wood existed; today, they import millions of board feet a year.

The growing popularity of cherry at home and abroad worries me greatly. I fear the stock of 70- to 120-year-old logs on which we depend will vanish in two decades or so. I am fanatical about using the wood efficiently; every month at our production meeting, I insist that we increase the percentage of number-one common-grade cherry that we use. The grade is cheaper to buy than FAS, but it is more expensive for us to use because we must expend more time and labor to cut out knots, wane, splits, and other imperfections. But cherry will not last if furniture makers use only the finest grade.

Beyond that, I feel that our best conservation effort is to create the finest, most durable, most beautiful, and most timeless furniture that we can. Quite simply, the wood is so precious and so threatened that it is a crime to make ugly or impermanent things from it. Our furniture is crafted to last for well over a century, but frankly I believe some pieces, with care, could last five hundred years or more. That is a long horizon, but cherry deserves no less.

Chapter 3
THE MOSER AESTHETIC

What is the Moser style? While I can recognize our company's pieces anywhere, I have never arrived at a shorthand label for our design philosophy. Others have called it transitional, postindustrial, organic, minimalist, neo-Shaker, and, oddly enough, both traditional and contemporary. The best course might be to avoid categorizing altogether. But since certain characteristics and influences of the Moser aesthetic can be pinned down, it seems worthwhile to attempt a definition.

Every design we make is rooted in a basic preference for simplicity of form, precise craftsmanship, and respect for natural materials. If power corrupts, so does artistry. Fine woodworking has been characterized as the art of hiding mistakes, and that is too often true. Stains, paint, gilding, lacquer, and veneers are usually ways of concealing inferior design, workmanship, and/or materials of dubious quality. An ancient Greek school of philosophy advocated sophistry, which celebrated deceit; the Sophists "made the worst appear better," a principle not lost on most modern manufacturers of furniture. Too often what you see is not real wood or real joinery, but a shell, one-fiftieth of an inch thick, hiding fake wood and screwed butt joints. From the very beginning, we have dedicated ourselves to avoiding such concealment; hence, simplicity, integrity in construction, and a love and respect for materials are expressed not only on the inside but on the exterior of a finished piece.

Opposite: The New Gloucester Rocker at home in an early house.
Above: The Crescent End Table, a new design advancing the curve.

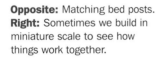

Scoop Seat Stool

But how does one take these fundamental personal preferences and translate them into furniture? Creativity, according to some people, should be synonymous with originality. Infused with divine inspiration, the artist should conjure objects *ex nihilio*. According to this way of thinking, the best preparation for making wonderful furniture would be to identify general aesthetic preferences, and then to dream up designs in an intellectual vacuum, unfettered by tradition. In the college-level design courses I have taught, I found this attitude common. Students paid little or no attention to historical forms, apparently fearing their creativity might be stifled.

I strongly disagree. The best designers, and I have known many, are avid students of the history of design. They synthesize and improve, but they always work within a framework of forms that has existed for decades, even centuries. Just as the best novelists must first master the language, the best wooden-furniture designers must first steep themselves in the vocabulary of historic styles, joinery, proportion, wood-species characteristics, finishing, and dozens of other arts, many of which were highly evolved centuries ago. It is no coincidence that

Opposite: Matching bed posts.
Right: Sometimes we build in miniature scale to see how things work together.

George Nakashima

No craftsman has had a greater influence on our evolution than George Nakashima. Born of Japanese parents in Spokane, Washington, in 1905, his early training as an architect led him to create furniture that fused the best of traditional American and Japanese aesthetics. He was thoroughly acquainted with the Windsor chair of the eighteenth and nineteenth centuries, but he saw it through the lens of a Japanese master. In the 1950s, at his shop in New Hope, Pennsylvania, he strove to give wood what he called a "second life" by celebrating its untamed forms, a reflection of the Japanese reverence for nature. He built tables and chests along early American lines, but used planks with sapwood and live edges still visible. He respected wood's tendency to crack, securing boards from further spread with his signature butterfly key. George proved that new design could flow from a synthesis of vastly different points of view, an idea that lies at the very heart of our work.

I visited his shop on three occasions, and I was impressed by his bearing as much as his furniture. Woodworkers, like other artists, are often insecure, wondering if they are too mainstream, too avant-garde, too slow and meticulous, too fast and sloppy, and so on. George was self-assured, full of a quiet conviction that he was on the right path, and his craftsmanship was flawless.

George's originality influenced not only us but also several generations of woodworkers, particularly on the West Coast. His sensitivity to materials led directly to what some call the California Organic school, later made famous by Art Carpenter and Sam Maloof. Though he died in 1990, his studio is still operated by his daughter, Mira Nakashima-Yarnell.

But it was not only George's designs that inspired us. He and his wife, Marion, showed that a family could build furniture with absolute integrity and make a successful small business from the endeavor. Throughout his life, his vision never faltered, his love of wood informed all that he did, and he embodied everything a designer-craftsman of wooden furniture aspires to be.

"It is an art- and soul-satisfying adventure to walk the forests of the world, to commune with trees . . . to bring this living material to the work bench, ultimately to give it a second life." —George Nakashima

most world-class furniture designers are all at least fifty years old. It takes nearly a lifetime to learn enough to do it well.

History will judge whether I am a good designer, but I am certainly well versed in traditional furniture design and construction. The library in which I write these words holds some two hundred volumes on the subject. I have read them all, and many, many more that have slipped through my hands but dwell in my unconscious. I have pursued and questioned the modern masters of wooden-furniture design, including Sam Maloof, George Nakashima, Hans Wegner, and innumerable others. I have taken apart hundreds of pieces of old furniture and then rebuilt

them, seeking to understand why they were made as they were. In restaurants, hotels, and the homes of friends, I have embarrassed my family countless times by crawling under tables, flipping over chairs, removing drawers, opening lids, prying back moldings, lifting mattresses, perusing the backsides of cases, and generally peering shamelessly into the dark and hidden recesses of furniture. When I can't spy sufficiently in situ, I buy. The staff at our shop expects to receive crates packed with tables, chairs, and chests purchased whenever I travel. Our business has a stock of international furniture— antiques and reproductions, one-of-a-kind and factory-made—that rivals collections I have seen in some museums.

My studies have not been confined to furniture. Any built object can fascinate, and its influence can creep into our work in unexpected ways. Three years ago, we decided to begin a line we came to call Sophia. The idea was to create a wooden sofa. It would have leather-upholstered seat cushions, but the arms and back would consist of curved wooden panels, sculpted to fit the natural contour of the lower back. The daunting challenge was joining a curved arm and a curved back to a straight leg. After much feverish sketching and cogitating, my son David and I came up with a triangular corner block, which transformed a square corner into a more graceful, curved turn. Three months later, I was shocked to realize that almost exactly the same structure, known as an

Left: Alvar Alto, the Finnish architect and furniture designer, experimented with curved laminations in birch. He taught us how to achieve the strength of steel with the warmth of wood. This leg joint, suggestive of a gothic column, is one of the most pleasing joints known to man.
Opposite: The Washington Square Chair. The design owes much to Frank Lloyd Wright and to Gerrit Rietveld, the turn-of-the-twentieth-century artist.

"I was shocked to realize that almost exactly the same structure, known as an architectural pendentive, had been used more than a thousand years ago to join the domed roof to the square base at the Hagia Sophia in Istanbul."

architectural pendentive, had been used more than a thousand years ago to join the domed roof to the square base at the Hagia Sophia in Istanbul. Did I reinvent the form? Maybe, but I believe a hypnotherapy session or two would reveal that I had observed and filed away that visual transition years ago. The inspiration for the back of the bow-back stool is none other than the seat of a Harley-Davidson motorcycle, specifically, the curved chrome bar that supported the passenger's back on a 1950s "buddy seat" (it was also gripped with white knuckles as the hapless passenger held on for dear life).

In short, everything that I have learned tends to impress itself upon our furniture as it moves from concept to reality. Years ago, a friend called our work "historical ambiguous." Though offered in a humorous and offhand way, his assessment was altogether accurate.

From the start, however, many of our designs came partially or wholly from employees, not me. During the 1970s, my workbench stood next to that of Chris Becksvoort, who came to Maine from Silver Spring, Maryland. Chris had worked closely with his father, a German-trained master woodworker. Although he majored in forestry, his passion was for hand tools and what could be achieved through their skilled use. Chris was a consummate technician and was instrumental in creating what has become our joint and construction vocabulary; today, he runs his own custom furniture shop in New Gloucester. Another colleague, Bill Huston, originally from Xenia, Ohio, graduated from a Norwegian trade school with an emphasis on woodworking and Scandinavian design. His aesthetic and work ethic left its mark during our thirteen-year association, and it continues to reverberate even today. Bill, Chris, and many others on the shop floor contributed to what has become our identifiable form.

But furniture design is not driven solely by style. The fundamental design criterion for any piece of furniture is the size and shape of the human body. It does not matter, for example, if a chair is Shaker, Chippendale,

Opposite: Fitting the triangle that completes the joint in the Sophia couch.

Danish modern, or injection-molded Jetsons plastic, the seat must be about eighteen inches above the floor, and there must be roughly twenty-one inches between the arms. Chair arms must fit under the standard thirty-inch-high tabletop, and the whole object must be light enough to be easily moved. Making too-faithful reproductions can get one into trouble. For example, the average American male today is about five feet ten inches tall, while in 1790 he was about five feet six inches. Furniture built in ignorance of or indifference to human-body proportions will not work, no matter how carefully it is otherwise designed or crafted.

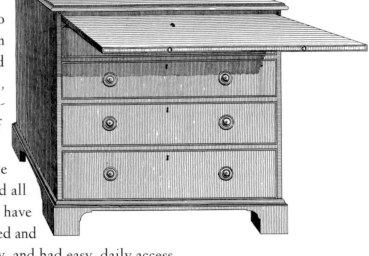

The perfect piece of furniture, then, to me, is one that respects the material from which it is made, fits the human body, and is comfortable, durable, and archetypal, giving the impression that adding, subtracting, or changing the proportions of any element would make it worse.

Early on, it seemed sensible to make Shaker reproductions, as the Shakers based all of their designs on precisely the criteria I have laid out. It was also logical because we lived and worked at the edge of a Shaker community, and had easy, daily access to their aesthetic. New Gloucester's Sabbathday Lake Shaker Village, founded in 1783, was, and still is, the country's only remaining active Shaker community. Although its chief contribution to the Shaker legacy was agricultural, a number of fine examples of wooden craftsmanship survive. The last male Shaker, Delmar Wilson, had a passion for oval boxes, and built five hundred each winter until his death in the early 1960s. The Sabbathday Lake Shaker Village remains very much intact, and includes a 1776 meetinghouse, residences, barns, and outbuildings furnished in original nineteenth-century fashion.

When we lived and worked near the community in the seventies and early eighties, the six remaining Shakers made baskets, prints, crafts, and herb products. But principally, I was intoxicated by the nineteenth-century Shaker furniture, perfectly preserved and in use even

Above: A four-drawer chest with shelf from George Hepplewhite's book, *The Cabinet-Maker and Upholsterer's Guide*, 1794. **Opposite:** Early doodlings occasionally result in finished furniture, but usually not. **Following pages:** Detail of New Gloucester Rocker.

Captain's Chair

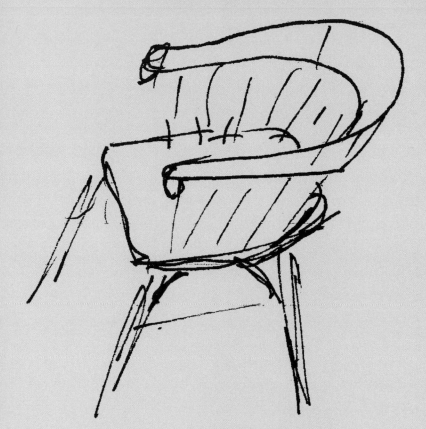

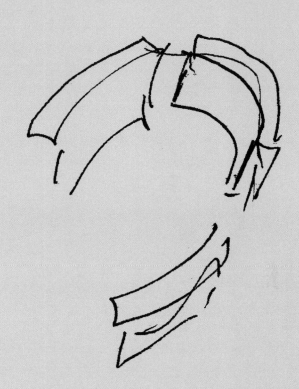

Martha Washington Chair

today. To me, it is deeply mysterious that such masterful, graceful, even spiritual objects could come from these largely unschooled people. Economy, unity, practicality, and proportion all merge into beauty that transcends culture and nationality; indeed, Shaker design, I have discovered in my European and Japanese travels, is more highly revered in those lands than it is in the United States. The impetus behind these works must, quite simply, have been God. A life force greater than the personal worked through these people.

Still, even in the early days, we did not copy Shaker work blindly. Obviously, no such thing as a Shaker entertainment center exists, so I made one according to my interpretation of how a Shaker would have made it. In addition, Shaker works were not our only influence, even at the very start of our business. Many people don't realize that the Shakers, for all of their ascetic separatism, came out of a larger nineteenth-century culture. Non-Shaker American furniture pieces of the same time, styles that are today called country Chippendale, country Hepplewhite, or country Sheraton, also influenced our work. All of these forms were, in turn, rooted in traditional English design, which is only

Opposite: Detail of Blanket Box with drawer.
Right: Detail of finger joint on a Shaker oval box.

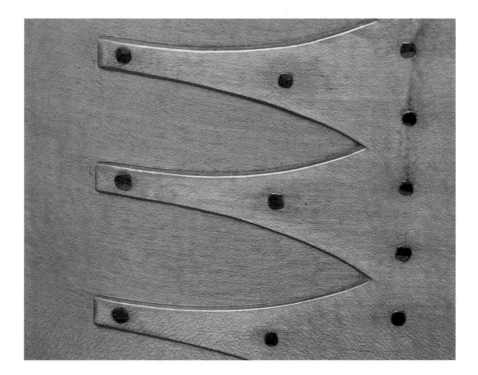

"If I had to link our furniture to any one tradition, it would be that of the skilled American nineteenth-century rural cabinetmaker—including the Shaker cabinetmaker—whose designs were rooted in utility, economy, and proportion, and who used the wood at hand, never mahogany, teak, or luan."

logical; early American settlers brought their tools, skills, and tastes along with them from Europe as a whole, and from England in particular.

Even today, if I had to link our furniture to any one tradition, it would be that of the skilled American nineteenth-century rural cabinetmaker —including the Shaker cabinetmaker—whose designs were rooted in utility, economy, and proportion, and who used the wood at hand, never mahogany, teak, or luan.

Another early influence was the Arts and Crafts movement. Oxford fine-arts professor John Ruskin contended that the factories of mid-nineteenth-century England, with their mind-numbing, repetitive tasks, were destroying humanity. Gordon Russell, a member of the peerage and a Ruskin devotee, created a furniture factory that was a sort of anti-factory, in which workers used hand tools and individual creativity was encouraged. The designs that emerged celebrated natural material (mostly English oak), eschewed superfluous decoration, and used joinery as ornament. In fact, Arts and Crafts workers sometimes intentionally deepened scribe marks, made joints self-consciously large,

Left: Blanket Box
Opposite: A door detail showing what we call a "spinner" lock. By turning the knob, the door locked to the vertical stile.

and installed hardware that was not just functional but oversized and of rough-hammered iron or copper.

While Ruskin and his cohorts were excessive on occasion, their ideals resonated with me, and in 1980, we began to incorporate visible joinery into our furniture—a departure from Shaker tradition, as the Shakers revealed joinery only sparingly. I firmly believe that design and structure should not occupy separate realms, that much of an object's beauty can and should spring from the structure that holds it together.

This idea is radical. With most furniture—in fact, with most of the built world—the purpose of design is to conceal structure. The trim around a bedroom door exists solely to hide the gap between the plaster and the door frame. That bit of "design" has no use but to hide the nails and shims that mate the door's casing to the house frame. Historically, the structure of most furniture has been similarly endoskeletal; that is, buried under the decorative flesh, almost as if the joinery that held the piece together and made it work was an embarrassment. This design philosophy reached a high—or low—point in the highly veneered surfaces characteristic of marquetry, where

Opposite: The McCain Library at Agnes Scott College in Decatur, Georgia. Installed in the spring of 2001, the tables are wired for laptops. This renovation was designed by Perry Dean Rogers and Partners of Boston.
Right: Detail of dovetails revealed on a case top.

This sideboard is derived from a Southern huntboard.

the point is not just to conceal structure but to conceal the fact that the object is furniture.

But Ruskin believed, and I do too, that hidden structure flies in the face of human nature. Human beings want to understand the workings of things they see. While we can certainly endure the uncertainty of how a dresser, a car, or a building is put together, the modern penchant for secreting structure leads, I think, to a mild neurosis. The return to popularity of timber framing stems from the

fact that we are more comfortable in a room with exposed beams, which serve as visual reassurance that the building won't collapse on our heads.

Hiding structure is also an affront to the craftsman. Furniture building is primarily an exercise in joinery. If the craftsman knows the finger joints, mortises, tenons, and other structural elements will all be hidden, the temptation is strong to make them quickly and sloppily, resulting in furniture that works poorly and falls apart readily. Conversely, the designer shows respect for the craftsman (or for him- or herself; if they are one in the same) by specifying visible joinery. A craftsman who is respected nearly always rises to the task, and is happy to do so.

So one of the first departures Moser furniture made from most traditional nineteenth-century pieces was to reveal and celebrate joinery. Visible dovetails join the sides and tops of our case work. We attach many of our chair legs with wedged through-tenons, so a quick glance assures the prospective sitter that the legs are firmly attached to the seat. Visible joinery, then, benefits everyone.

Danish design, specifically, the 1950s movement toward simplicity of form that came to be known as Danish modern, is another huge influence on our work. Many Americans don't realize that such Danish masters as Hans Wegner, Borge Mogensen, and Arne Jacobsen were the

Left: Molding detail. Using a sliding French dovetail, the miter joint of the top molding is always tight—the seasonal movement in the case is transferred to the back of the case.
Opposite: A very simple four-posted platform bed. Proportion means so much.

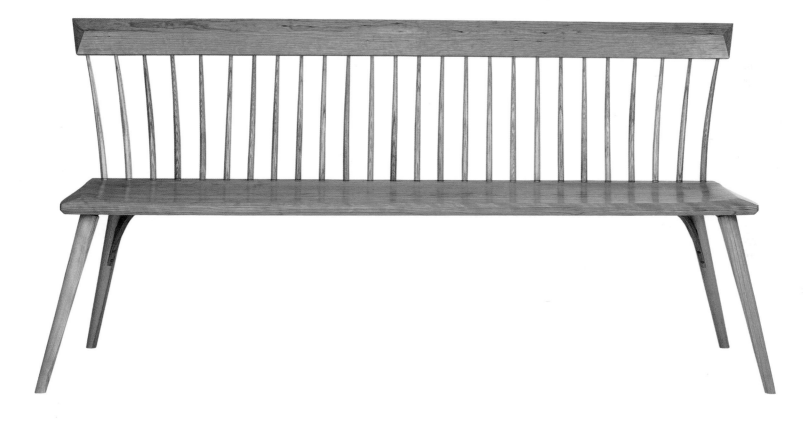

Opposite: Andy Moser using the jointer. **Above:** Eastward Bench.

first to discover, revere, and reinterpret American Shaker furniture. While Eisenhower-era Americans were burning Shaker ladderback chairs as old-fashioned junk, the Danes were shipping them home to study. In 1982, Mary and I went to the Scandinavian furniture fair in Denmark; we were the only American exhibitors there. Our largely reproduction work was well received, but I was more interested in the Danes' work than they were in mine. When I saw Wegner's wishbone chair—a stunning, minimalist design with its characteristic V-shaped back slat—and other Danish interpretations of Shaker forms, I had an epiphany. I turned to Mary and said, "That's what we need to do." When we returned to Maine, we began even more earnestly to do with Moser furniture precisely what the Danes had already done: reinterpret Shaker furniture for a modern market.

The Danes also have an unmatched reverence for natural materials, even greater than that of the Shakers, who often painted their furniture. The Danes believe, as I do, that wood is more satisfying than chrome-plated steel or aluminum. Leather is more beautiful than plastic. Cotton, linen, and silk are superior to polyester. Oil and wax are more

Above: Cutting leather in the upholstery shop. Most upholstered furniture is ungainly; I have endeavored to make ours clean and spare.
Opposite: Detail of the Lolling Chair.

Opposite: Hand rasping the continuous arm. There is no way to automate this process. It takes about six months before a trainee can do it quickly and confidently. Some people never can master it. **Above:** As a youngster, Matthew became quite proficient on the lathe and turned many of the knobs for our early case pieces.

appealing than polyurethane. Despite the proliferation of synthetic materials, I believe that human beings feel uncomfortable around them because we don't have a history with them, and consequently we don't understand them. They are mysteries, and we are hardwired to equate mystery with danger. The longing for the natural materials with which we coevolved is welded to our DNA, and as we alienate ourselves more and more from the cottage and the cave, our yearning for the natural world grows stronger. Furniture made of natural materials nourishes not just our vision and touch but our ears as well. The New Gloucester rocker makes a subtle, muted squeak as it moves. I love the fact that it does. Now and then, a customer asks us to "fix" the squeak, but most customers assure me that I am not alone in my appreciation for the ancient sound of wood rubbing wood.

Perhaps due in part to my German ancestry, I am also an admirer of the Bauhaus movement, the general term for the design philosophy of the Staatliches Bauhaus, an industrial-arts school founded by architect Walter Gropius in the Weimar Republic in 1919. The mission of the school was to bring the clean, streamlined functionalism of the best of modern technology into the home. While I generally dislike the school's choice of materials—the cold, clinical chromed steel and glass of Bauhaus chairs, lamps, and other furnishings—I find the forms themselves delightful in their minimalism. To a large extent, our chaise lounge, introduced in 1999, traces to a similar chair made in the 1930s by Alvar Aalto, the Finnish architect who was heavily influenced by the Bauhaus sensibility.

Still, the business of tracking down influences can get dicey. I often say that I am a devotee of the work of Frank Lloyd Wright and of traditional Japanese design. Yet Wright himself was an indefatigable Japanophile, so if one likes Wright, does one like Wright or Japan? Many

Opposite: Harpswell Arm Chair, based on a French form of around 1950.
Right: Harpswell Side Chair.
Following pages: The Laptop Desk houses a laptop computer, printer, and fax machine. It is based on the laptop desks once used in stagecoaches and by Thomas Jefferson to write the Declaration of Independence.

"I often say that I am a devotee of the work of Frank Lloyd Wright and of traditional Japanese design. Yet Wright himself was an indefatigable Japanophile, so if one likes Wright, does one like Wright or Japan?"

years ago, the American wing of the Metropolitan Museum of Art in New York exhibited a roomful of stunning furniture Wright had designed for a Minneapolis home built in 1911. I marveled that anyone could possess the genius to create such utterly original yet harmonious forms. I discovered years later that these pieces were beautiful because they were so thoroughly Japanese. In 1998, my son Aaron and I had dinner in a samurai hotel in Kyoto, which was built in 1818; we were told we dined in the room in which Wright lived while studying Japanese architecture. The geometric shapes, the pattern of wood, void, wood, void, wood, void, so characteristic of Wright were in the paneling and furniture of that room. Today, the same sensibility is in

many of our furniture pieces, most notably in the double vertical that characterizes our Windward line of chairs and bookcases. The Prairie Home, icon of the Midwest, can be seen in seminal form at the Emperor's Summer Palace in Kyoto. Our work and Wright's work are parts of a long continuum of admiration, influence, and refinement.

Do all of these influences have a single source? In other words, is there a common thread that unites Wright, mission, Bauhaus, Arts and Crafts, and the rest, and that explains why we seem instinctively to find them appealing?

I think so, and the answer is nature herself. Nature is replete with economically engineered organic materials, and I believe each of my favorite schools of design attempts, consciously or otherwise, to replicate her feat. While man builds a concrete tower that fights the elements,

Left: A New Century Pedestal Extension Table, inspired by Arts and Crafts designs.
Right: The Japanese penchant for dividing space with vertical and horizontal elements influenced our New Century chair, just as it did Frank Lloyd Wright's prairie architecture.

The Sublime

One afternoon several years ago, I got a call from a *New York Times* writer who was doing a feature story on the nature of good design. I was one of five designers from diverse disciplines whom he interviewed, asking each of us to name the

most sublime object in our experience. It made me think. In this age of secular humanism, the word "sublime" has lost its spiritual dimensions, and references to heaven or the inspiration of God are often viewed with suspicion. But since "sublime" comes from the Latin *sublimis*, which means to elevate, I firmly believe that the word must connote transcendence of this lowly plane. In other words, that which is sublime must have benefited from God's participation.

It is easy to identify what aspires to the sublime in music (Mozart) or rhetoric (Churchill), but deciding upon a single object is more difficult. When asked, the architect cited buildings and the product designer invoked silver flatware. My mind's eye was flooded with images of an exquisite Queen Anne tea table, and the breathtaking five-faceted concave curve of an Alvar Aalto table leg. But at last, it came firmly to rest on an improbable object, one so mundane and commonplace that I was at first hesitant to offer it: a simple wooden pulley, built by an anonymous Shaker craftsman in the nineteenth century. I saw it in New York in 1985, as part of the Whitney Museum's *Shaker Design* exhibition. Responding to the journalist's question, I studied a wonderful

photo of the pulley taken by famed architectural photographer Paul Rocheleau.

The unknown Shaker artist showed tremendous respect for the wood with his delicate treatment of the body, complete with gentle chamfers and cyma curves. He did not just drill the rope tunnel; he vaulted it with a flourish. The iron portion, most likely shaped by a blacksmith, is similarly respectful, bracing only those few portions where wood would surely be inadequate. Economy of material is everywhere apparent: nothing to be added, nothing to remove. And all the while, this piece of transcendent art was not made to perch on a museum pedestal, but to serve, effectively unseen, as a tool. It did not have to be made nearly this well, as a much cruder block would still have guided the rope, but it was crafted with skill and passion and intelligence, and it radiates the maker's ultimate objective: to worship with his hands. To the Shakers, the values of unity, utility, economy, and reverence for materials were truly a prayerful offering to God. All of them came together in that pulley.

Left: A nineteenth century Shaker pulley.
Opposite: Good design should be at home in a variety of settings. Here is our work in a truly historic environment.

nature grows a slender tree that bends with the wind—and is more likely than any tower to be left standing after a hurricane. A bird, a butterfly, a spider web—each is constructed of the precise minimum required to do the job well, and not an ounce more. Function, not superfluous ornament, is the criterion by which nature designs. The best furniture design considers first what the object must do. If an object is functional, it is generally beautiful as well. We are all born with an innate ability to recognize and appreciate the design genius that is born of nature, of a system in which whatever does not work is recalled by the manufacturer, with no chance for appeal. The best designs take nature for their inspiration; in fine woodworking, it is the common root, literally and figuratively.

Nonetheless, it is important not to get carried away with a purely intellectual understanding of design and its influences. Reading books, studying furniture, and even studying nature do not fully explain what goes into designing new furniture, at least not for me. I have found that how one creates—the physical act itself—has a major influence upon what one creates.

Left: A cabinetmaker scribing in the leaf of a brass hinge.

Borrowings

Rarely does design flow from spontaneous imagination. That notion, though romantic, is actually a prescription for works that range from substandard to dreadful. Conversely, a designer who depends upon historical precedent builds on the accumulated wisdom and success of countless talented men and women, and so enjoys a much greater chance of creating beauty and utility. Mostly, we design from fully

formed antecedents, well fixed in memory though prone to dwell below the threshold of conscious recall. An example of my subconscious borrowing is the ribbon-like handrail of a spiral staircase at the Shaker Community in Pleasant Hill, Kentucky. I've known about this rail for a long time, but saw it firsthand only three years ago. The shape from photographs has been with me much longer, and it found its way into a love seat

that I designed and built twenty-five years ago.

Not all borrowings spring from aesthetics. Some forms are dictated by natural law. Gravity is the enemy of anything made to sit in or upon. The stress of a two-hundred-pound body on a fragile chair frame can be overwhelming. There are two approaches to strengthening a chair: one is through mass, as in the case of a box frame chair, which is akin to a Roman aqueduct; the other is through tension, as in the case of a Windsor chair, which is akin to a suspension bridge. While mass, and box frames, certainly have their place, I confess I prefer the elegance of the Windsor, and I depended heavily on that antecedent when designing our Continuous Arm Chair. Drop a box frame chair from a three-story window and it will likely break; drop a Continuous Arm Chair and it will likely bounce. These may seem like unlikely events, but in a two-hundred-year lifespan, every chair will be stressed in unique ways.

A Windsor chair prevails because it flexes under pressure. However, this characteristic is not immediately evident from the chair's appearance. It looks fragile. We sit with our eyes, and we equate strength with mass. In this assumption, we are often mistaken.

Usually in industrial society, the designer and the craftsman are different people. This is understandable, as there is often a difference in temperament between the two. Generally, the designer is part of the educational elite, and is happy to live in a world of intellectual forms and ideas. He or she often lacks motor skills, and, further, is rather proud of that fact. Indeed, the worst designers are often contemptuous of the "manual laborer" who actually does the work.

The craftsman, on the other hand, takes pleasure in the physical process of marrying piece to piece, of the sensory richness of the sight, smell, and sound of building. But he or she may have little or no interest in design, and is happy to leave that part of the creative process to the designer.

I have had the good fortune to love both aspects of furniture creation, and if there is an unusual sense of unity of design and construction in our work, it is because—in the early days, anyway—the designer and the constructor were often the same person. I love to design furniture, but I also love to stand at a lathe or a drill press for hours on end.

The advantage of these fortunate proclivities is that I can, and do, design primarily by building rather than drawing. To design a new chair, I will often build a dozen or more chairs, sitting in each one, seeing how well it works or does not work. The processes of designing and building are, for me and increasingly for my son David, impossible to tease apart. We have plans for all of our pieces, but they are nearly always drawn after the prototype is built, not before.

While designing-by-building is tedious and slow, the great advantage is that the tools and wood become collaborators, constantly informing us of what will work and what won't, and actually suggesting ideas that we would never imagine if confined to a drawing board or, worse, a computer screen. In building, the craftsman is constantly adjusting dimension, shadow, balance, often with materials that happen to be at hand, which leads to serendipity. Much brilliance results from historical accident. An artist runs out of red but keeps painting; the tools and materials guide him or her in a better direction because of the deficiency.

Opposite: Oval Ring Extension Table.
Following pages: The design studio at Dingley Island. The shop usually isn't this clean.

136

A great deal of ugliness exists in the built world today. Some of it can be traced to a widespread ignorance of history, to a tendency by modern designers to place originality above utility and beauty. But I believe the modern rift between designer and craftsman is the greatest cause behind the creation of jarring, inharmonious, impractical, impermanent objects. If I were dean of a school of architecture, I would require my students to work summers as welders, bricklayers, framers, and trim carpenters, to get their hands dirty in the creation of the kinds of things that they aspire to design. And if I were a job-site foreman, I would urge my carpenters to think like designers, daring them to veer from the blueprint if their experience tells them that the object they are building is not as good as it could be, and to create new works out of their own knowledge if the spirit moves them to do so. A little anarchy in the building process is stimulating.

But most of all, I hope more and more people will regard themselves as neither designers nor builders but both. It is from these people that the best designs have tended to come, and will for eternity.

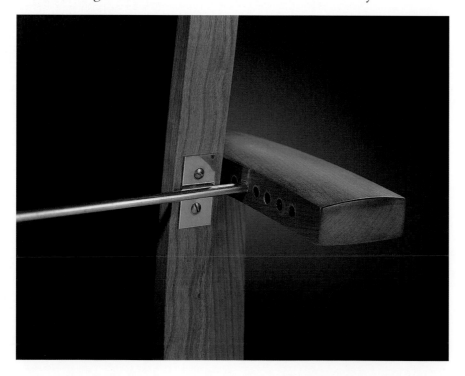

Left: Close-up of adjusting device for the Lolling Chair. **Opposite:** David Moser and Warren Shaw collaborating in the prototype shop. We try to make our designs look "right," as if they could be no other way. This happens not through divine inspiration, but a painstaking process of sketching, building, evaluating, and building again. The chaise lounge, for example, took an entire year of prototype work to perfect.

Opposite: Lila Smith constructing a chair subassembly. **Above:** Drawer side detail. The front is cherry; the sides and bottom are ash.

Chapter 4
CRAFTSMANSHIP

To me, the means of making furniture is often more interesting than the furniture itself. Any woodworker will agree that there are multiple ways to create a particular furniture part, or to connect one part to another (woodworkers were called joiners for a reason). Each piece can be cut, carved, curved, sanded, and finished by a variety of hand and machine tools. Joinery methods are legion: a corner, for example, can be dovetailed, butted, box jointed, rabbeted, mitered, lock jointed, doweled, mortise-and-tenoned (and a half-dozen kinds of mortise-and-tenon joints are possible), pocket screwed, biscuited, splined, and more. The curve in a round table's apron can be steam bent, flitch cut and glue laminated, or sawn from a wide plank. New woodworking technologies are birthed seemingly every week, with more and more tools computer-controlled, and new cutting technologies such as lasers replacing age-old metal blades.

How do we decide which method to use? Typically, the management of a furniture factory will begin by purchasing a collection of industrial woodworking equipment. Company designers will then design the furniture around the means of production, aiming to maximize machine efficiency and minimize the need for skilled manual labor, which is scarce and expensive. This is a highly cost-effective practice; without it, the

Opposite: A chisel is used to trim the pin flush to the frame. The pin locks in the tenon as a precaution against glue failure, which will most certainly occur as the years pass.
Above: Six Drawer Dresser

thirty-nine-dollar Taiwan-made pseudo-Windsors sold by Wal-Mart would be impossible. But it is also a slippery slope that leads to inferior furniture. I once toured a ready-made cabinet factory in which no human being touched the product from beginning to end. Machines arrayed along moving belts independently did all cutting and assembly, resulting in cabinets that were weak, monotonous, and ugly, but profitable to sell and cheap to purchase. History shows that the best furniture happens when the designer creates the finest forms that he or she can, then adapts the means of production to accommodate that design. In short, the furniture should come first.

On the other hand, we can't turn our backs completely on production efficiency. Only in a decadent society can a high-end studio furniture designer-maker spend a thousand hours handcrafting a fifty-thousand-dollar desk, a frivolity for the elite few. Such excess reminds me of the worst of czarist Russia, where a Fabergé egg made for the czarina's fancy had a value equal to the homes of one thousand peasants. We could, theoretically, use nothing but hand tools to produce our furniture, but prices would soon multiply, placing the furniture out of the reach of

Left: Empire style describes a neo-classical period following the exploits of Napoleon. Ancient Greece inspired the style, which in turn inspired the Island Chair shown here. It is our first serious venture into the use of woven cane.
Opposite: A bedside stand with drawer and shelf.

all but the extremely wealthy. Further, the furniture would be no better. In some ways, it would be worse.

Instead, we have always engaged in a delicate balance, seeking to find the best way to build a given piece of furniture that involves no compromise in aesthetics or structural integrity. Most of our operations have evolved significantly over thirty years, yet we have never made a change that sacrificed quality for the sake of efficiency. In every case, a faster method was used only if the resulting product was as good or better than what it replaced.

Take, for example, the scooped seat of the Continuous Arm Chair. This is similar to the seat of the nineteenth-century Windsor chair, gently contoured to cradle the sitter's hindquarters. Carving the twin depressions, which range from five-eighths to three-quarters inches below the surface plane of the wood and are divided by a ridge called the pumel, is among the most complex and challenging traditional furniture operations—a process more akin to sculpting than woodworking. The seat is typically made from a shield-shaped slab of glued-up wood two inches thick. The woodworker uses a hollowing tool called a gutter adze to scoop out the bulk of the material, then employs a variety of specialized tools to smooth and refine the depression, including inshaves, scorps, curved spokeshaves known as travishers, compass planes, and, ultimately, scrapers.

These seats were traditionally made of pine or poplar because hollowing out hardwood with hand tools is exceptionally difficult. For this reason, we used northern white pine and hand tools in the early days, but when we switched to cherry, we knew we had to change the system, as cherry is roughly twice as hard as white pine and nearly impossible to shape this way.

We quickly evolved a system using the table saw. We lowered the blade, placed the chair seat over it, then slowly raised the blade while turning the seat in a jig to create a pair of bowl-like depressions.

Then we used a drill press to bore a series of holes at various depths along the top front of the slab. With the holes as guides, we used a chain saw to rough out the hollows where the thighs rest.

But, myriad problems arose with these tool choices. First, spinning a chair seat on the slowly raised blade of a table saw is dangerous; the lateral pressure can make the blade suddenly grab the wood and send it flying. Second, a chain saw is a crude finishing tool. The saw tends to grab the wood and shoot forward, ruining the seat.

The first major advance we made was the purchase of a 1950s routing machine designed to mold oval picture frames. It was essentially a Jeffersonian pantograph with a router, instead of a quill pen, at the production end. We adapted it to shape a chair seat: the woodworker, moving the stylus over a completed seat, automatically piloted the router-bearing end over a blank, making a rough copy. This system was not only more accurate than our former method, but it was also far safer, as the woodworker never came closer than two feet from the spinning router blade. Still, it was slow and tedious work.

Then, in 1984, I read about a computer-guided industrial machine called a core cutter that cut the wings of fighter aircraft out of a huge block of honeycombed magnesium foil. No two square inches of a fighter-wing surface have the same orientation to the centerline of the wing, so this shape had been a huge challenge to machine by hand. But the core cutter sports a router-type bit on three full and two partial axes, allowing it to carve virtually any three-dimensional shape, no matter how irregular. I went out to the Thermwood company in Indiana, and asked if the same five-axis Cartesian technology could be used to

Above: Driving a wedge into a leg tenon. There is no gauge that tells the woodworker how long or hard to pound, but it must be done correctly. Too much or too little are equally disastrous. Sound and resistance provide subtle clues that require experience to recognize. **Opposite:** Our five-axis Cartesian router.

The Seton Hall Chair

You cannot flip through the *New Yorker* without encountering advertisements for ergonomic chairs, each one promising to be more effective than the last. Since most of us spend endless hours seated at a work-station of some sort, the lower back, the neck, and the carpal tunnel of the wrist all too often wind up as victims of this twenty-first-century occupational position. Ergonomics is the science of molding the material world to accommodate the human body, and it is a vast and diverse field of inquiry; no doubt one can get a Ph.D. in it. Experts write volumes on the subject, and laboratories endlessly test theories, many of them centered on chair design.

In the absence of such a laboratory at our shop, we were at a loss to determine the best design for a three-position library chair that we agreed to design for Seton Hall University. The university was building a new library and needed several hundred chairs to accommodate everyone who might use the facility. Specifically, these chairs needed to

serve readers, who like to lean back; keyboardists, who want support when angled forward; and people who like a position somewhere in between. In short, we were hired to create the ultimate ergonomic library chair.

We built a low box-frame chair with a sled base. We sent the chair, along with a small collection of premeasured wooden wedges, to the monsignor's office, and he tried different combinations of wedges until he arrived at three flat faces of the base

that angled the chair to his satisfaction. These angles became the template for the official Seton Hall chair. This was an exercise in pragmatism; the research combined commonsense prototyping and customer participation in a way that made everyone happy. As usual, a successful chair design proved to be the result of sitting in and fiddling with a real chair, rather than dreaming up and drawing ethereal ones.

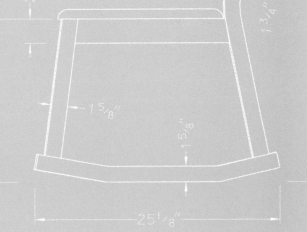

2 1/2"

1 5/16"

13 1/4"

38 3/8"

17"

1 5/8"

1 5/8"

25 1/8"

SIDE VIEW

Opposite: An occasional chair using brass, leather, and cane. **Following pages:** The leg parts are for a Lolling Chair.

shape chair seats and drill holes for spindles. They said if it could cut the curve in an aircraft wing, it should be able to do the same for a chair seat. We bought it in 1987, and it was a huge step for us.

It was also perhaps the most controversial action we have ever taken. When purists survey our operation, they point to that machine as emblematic of compromise.

My response is two-fold. First, we create a wide variety of sculptured forms, many more than most furniture companies. We simply had to find a way to make this process faster, safer, and more accurate, or we could no longer sell furniture at a profit and grow as a company.

Second, and more importantly, handwork remains a substantial part of our operation, so much so that apologies seem foolish. The workbenches that our assemblers use today are exactly the same ones that we used in the early days in New Gloucester, when our operation was primitive by any standard. Today, our Dr. White's chest, the most complex piece we create, can take up to fifty hours simply to assemble. All fifty hours are spent in meticulous, skilled handwork.

In general, my philosophy has been to seek the fastest possible way to make parts consistent with quality and safety. Any high-tech cutting and shaping machinery that we can afford and that does the job well, we will have. Then, we rely exclusively on skilled hand labor to put the pieces together. While machine assembly of wooden furniture is possible, we use no machines. Our assembly system is so primitive that visitors from other furniture companies leave scratching their heads. The notion that our drawers are so unstandardized that they can't be swapped out, that you cannot take a drawer from one case and put it into another, boggles them. An even more dramatic example of the variability of hand labor is the fact that George Colby, whose job, among others, is to shape the complex arm of the Continuous Arm Chair with a ten-inch rasp, can tell who worked on a given arm just by looking at it.

In short, there must be some efficiency or we fail, but there must be some inefficiency, or we also fail. We have to plan inefficiency into the operation, which should result in spontaneity, irregularity, and exuberance. British designer and architect David Pye, in his book *The*

Nature and Art of Workmanship, calls the kind of work we do "the manufacture of risk." As he put it, this type of manufacturing is characterized by "any kind of technique or apparatus [tool] in which the quality of the result is not predetermined, but depends on the judgment, dexterity and care which the maker exercises as he works. The essential idea is that the quality of the result is continually at risk during the process of making." In other words, when you begin, you are not exactly sure what the object is going to look like because you have allowed chance and choice to be part of the everyday production process. Manufacturing becomes infused with humanity, so the pieces produced reflect how the craftsman felt the morning when he or she pounded in the last wedge, or whether the board split when an operation was attempted, which then required the sawing off of a half inch and a new start. When the worker spends fifty hours assembling a piece, literally thousands of challenges arise that require a reaction, and no two craftsmen will react in the same way.

Perhaps the greatest variable between two craftsmen is the level of experience. Whenever we have hired new people, I have gravitated more toward those with little or no woodworking experience but a sense of enthusiasm about life and pride in what they do. The inexperienced can be taught—indeed, it is generally better to teach

it fresh than to have people "unlearn" poor woodworking habits—but the enthusiasm and pride seem largely innate. As in the traditional journeyman system, people in our shop serve long apprenticeships in the most repetitive aspects of production, such as sanding and finishing, generally needing several years to graduate to the more demanding tasks of parts production and assembly. But once they achieve that level, they tend to stay. Our turnover rate among master craftsmen is about 3 percent.

Opposite: Some of our fixtures are not simply tools for making art, they are art. Jared Smith builds them.
Right: Wanda Ray putting on wax.
Following pages: Continuous Arm Chair with Writing Desk.

We are unique among woodworking operations in that we hire large numbers of women. Most Danish shops I have toured have had no female floor-workers at all, but roughly 40 percent of our craftsmen are female. Although there are many exceptions, I have found that women are generally more patient and more detail oriented than men, and are consequently a great asset in the sanding and finishing departments, but the fact is, they can excel anywhere. For eight years, a woman ran our parts department, and she had twenty-three people, mostly men, reporting to her.

Through the years, I've had three careers: first as a college professor, second as a craftsman, and third as a businessman. Despite the progression, I have never stopped teaching. Woodworking cannot be

"It is a constant delight to watch woodworking cross social divides in our shop, to see high-school dropouts and Ph.D.'s bond over a common love of wood. To this day, the teaching works in both directions; I learn something every week from people in the shop."

learned successfully from books. The best instruction takes place shoulder to shoulder, stroke to stroke, face to face. While I take great pleasure in creating wooden objects, the thrill of teaching—in a sense, "creating"—woodworkers has been my predominant joy of the last decade or so. It is a constant delight to watch woodworking cross social divides in our shop, to see high-school dropouts and Ph.D.'s bond over a common love of wood. To this day, the teaching works in both directions; I learn something every week from people in the shop.

In the 1990s, we increasingly transitioned into more curvilinear forms. They are an order of magnitude more difficult to create than the rectilinear pieces on which we forged our early reputation, but the challenge has served to keep us sharp. At one time, our designs were so simple that virtually every town in America had a woodworker of sufficient skill to duplicate them. Indeed, many have tried. Small

Left: The Chaise Lounge shown in two positions.
Opposite: The Chaise Lounge

woodworking shops are increasingly copying our early designs inch for inch and dovetail for dovetail. With the introduction of our curved-front Crescent cabinets, and especially with the advent of our lolling chair and chaise lounge, I can confidently state that the average one-man shop would have considerable difficulty replicating those forms.

Why are we doing this? On a basic level, we are expanding our product line to attract a wider sphere of customers. Our earlier pieces were seen as too angular and masculine for some people; the curved forms, with a more feminine feel, may draw the once uninterested. But on another level, we make these for the same reason that a professional athlete tries to run faster, a short-story writer tackles a novel, or anyone

Opposite: The Bowfront Chest is a twenty-first-century interpretation of a Hepplewhite version two hundred years its senior.
Right: Cindy Morin readies a chair for the finishing room.

Left: From left: Aaron, our number three son, officially joined the company in 1991 and is responsible for library and corporate sales; Mary, co-founder; David, the last born, began in 1989 and runs the prototype shop; myself, I have no job description; Andrew, began in 1987 and works in the shop; and, Matthew, our oldest son, who worked with us from 1982 to 1999 and now runs his own cabinet shop in the old Grange Hall in New Gloucester, Maine.

Opposite: The Washington Square Chair was first envisioned as useful sculpture. Though higher than this and with a wooden plank seat it did not look comfortable—but in this case appearances are wrong. The shorter version of the chair shown here populates the Van Pelt Library at the University of Pennsylvania and is appreciated for its comfort and utility.

who is passionate about anything tries to move to a higher level of difficulty. Simply put, it is human nature to strive, to explore what can be done. I believe that human beings are, by nature, thing makers, and those of us who are lucky enough to have occupations that reflect this basic human urge will eventually, inevitably, try to stretch and grow and make a better thing. Finally, exploring new levels of difficulty is invariably fun.

Are we succeeding? Success is not an end point. Thos. Moser Cabinetmakers has been a process rather than a static entity since the day of its founding. I expect that process to continue.

The House on Dingley Island

The largest piece of furniture I ever designed sits on a rocky point of Dingley Island, about five miles south of Brunswick, Maine. It is the house that Mary and I built from 1992 to 1995, and the one in which we now live. While houses are generally built to a differing set of standards than woodworking pieces, most of this one is not: the

tolerances, materials, finishes, and much of the joinery are identical to what comes out of our shop.

Like the best furniture, our house is designed from the inside out, the idea being that if an object serves its occupants well, beauty will arise organically. The only thought Mary and I gave to the outer form was that it would be a variant of the New England cape, and would hunker fairly low on the

landscape, unlike the towering eyesores that some feel compelled to build on rocky points in Maine.

Like the best furniture, the house looks inevitable, but was, in fact, far from it. I agonized over every detail just as I agonize over every aspect of our furniture. I am not Mozart, taking dictation from God; I am Salieri, scratching out, revising, storming away in disgust, and returning with humility and resolve to do it right this time. If I am a better furniture designer than Salieri was an opera composer—and only history will judge if that is true—it is because I keep trying long after he would have decided a particular passage was good enough.

The tempestuous tale of the house's construction is written in the rat's nest of drawings in a drawer in our boathouse (which

was the first structure we built here, and the place we inhabited while constructing the main house). Scrawled on these papers— some are literally the backs of envelopes— are myriad details: a stair-rail profile, the covered porch's dimensions, stile-and-rail spacings in the study's wainscoting, and on and on. Incredibly, this morass of drawn musings constitutes the totality of the house plans. An architect who saw this—I assure you, none ever did—would shriek and faint, but this is how I have always worked. Rough sketch, then build, then rough sketch again, then build again, the processes informing each other, and me, of what works and what doesn't. It is slow, clumsy, expensive, and exasperating to all of those around me, and if I could do it another way, I would. But I can't.

Far left: Standing on the oceanside of the house. I never know whether this is the frontyard or the backyard. **Left:** Mary and I wake up every morning with the sun. Not a day has gone by without seeing some wildlife appearing. **Opposite:** The studio workshop, or what we call the barn. This dramatic photograph has everything in it, even the photographer Paul Rocheleau.

I wanted the house to celebrate the joiner's art, and it does. The first floor's ceiling is paneled in walnut coated with linseed oil and beeswax, burnished to a rich luster. The floor picks up the glow. Made of one-hundred-year-old Burmese teak salvaged from the Rangoon River and cured in my shop for three years, it evokes the deck of some lovingly crafted sailboat.

On the south wall of the living room, where some might have installed a great "picture window" to gawk at the view, I set three smaller windows side by side and placed above them a divided-light transom. My aim was to frame the seascape rather than to hurl it indoors. A beautiful view through a smallish window is a framed, somewhat elusive delight; the same view through a large window quickly goes stale. Actually, the windows are still too big, and each summer, I threaten to remove them and start over.

The master bedroom is essentially a large bay window thrust out from the second floor, with room for our bed and little else. When we awake, the panorama of Dingley Cove, Sheep Island, and a spreading apple tree greet us through glass trimmed with cypress. We never shut the curtains, which imposes upon us the pleasant discipline of sleeping with the sun. If it is up at five, then so are we.

This is the house in which Mary and I hope to grow old. A day never passes here without a nod of appreciation for our good fortune. Like our furniture, the house will persist long after we are gone. I hope that it stays in the family—and with four sons and, at this writing, six grandchildren, there are plenty of Mosers who might literally assume the mantel. If not, I hope whoever lives here will, like us, feel blessed, and marvel at how life's twisting path led to this singular destination.

Chapter 5
SHOP TOUR

In my thirty years as a professional furniture maker, I have studied furniture shops as intensely as—often, more intensely than—I have studied furniture itself. A good shop, like good furniture, is elegant without ornament, a joy to use, adaptable to changing circumstance, durable, safe, easy to repair, and, frankly, beautiful.

Again like good furniture, good shops are built upon a foundation of tradition, upon years of study of what works and does not work in prior models. I have visited scores of furniture-making shops all over the world, from the chair-making studios of Udine, Italy, where 80 percent of Europe's wooden chairs are made, to the masters' shops in London's East End, to cabinetworks in Kyoto, Japan. I have even visited and studied the shop that makes the last surviving American mechanical clock, another that makes cotton sheets, another that makes reproduction lighting, and many more, looking for the common denominator that makes one manufacturing operation joyful, efficient, and profitable while another is dreary, wasteful, and probably doomed.

Our shop owes something to every successful shop I have seen, but it is most closely based on the Danish model. I have visited a dozen Danish furniture factories through the years, and have come to two conclusions: the Danes make the finest solid-wood furniture in the

Opposite: A collection of hand tools not gathered for effect but actually used daily by the folks in Assembly. Doors and drawers are fitted with tolerances based on the season (loose in the winter, tight in the summer). Every craftsman has his own tools. The chisel shown here has been sharpened by more than one generation of woodworkers.

Left: Cutting freehand is a skill that comes only with experience. The beginner carefully follows the line, always cutting on the waste side of the line so that if a mistake occurs it destroys that which will be sanded away in any case. The expert stays on the line and is lightening-fast.
Opposite: This thirty-six-inch bandsaw runs off of a direct drive slow RPM motor and is made of solid cast iron. With new rubber tires on the wheels and a new blade guide it operates without vibration and can run non-stop without overheating. Sometimes the old machines are the best.

world, and the best Danish furniture comes from shops with sixty to seventy production workers. Today, with our sixty-five craftsmen on the production floor, we are in the center of that sweet spot, and this is where I hope we will stay. In Denmark, when demand exceeds capacity, the Danes actually build another sixty-five-worker factory rather than attempt to expand an existing one, a move any American efficiency expert would protest as ruinously expensive. My response is that you do what you have to do to safeguard the craft. When an organization becomes so large that the workers cannot know each other by name, become friends, and freely discuss how to do the work well, the product suffers, as do the people who make it.

Like Danish shops, ours is organized in two distinct halves: parts production, on the north side of the building, and assembly and finish, on the south side. These areas are different in nearly every way: they look different, sound different, and are staffed by people of different temperaments. They even smell different.

The parts department is decidedly industrial, featuring concrete floors, humming machinery, repetitive tasks, and the smell of oil,

sawdust, and ozone. In general, this side attracts tough, physical, hardworking people.

This is the loading-dock side, where eighteen-wheel trucks, each bearing fifteen-thousand-board-feet of lumber, pull up to deliver their contents, and the forklift runs all day long. Lumber starts its journey toward furniture on this side, and here is where a man or woman might handle five hundred or a thousand boards in one day. This is also the point at which a job ticket is attached to a wheeled cart. The ticket informs all participants down the road of precisely what the piece requires, and includes the owner's name and shipping instructions.

Yet even here among the whirling blades and hissing pneumatic clamps, a good eye and a fine aesthetic sensibility are crucial. These people choose the lumber that will go into an individual piece, and they must possess a keen appreciation for how to match wood color and grain for an overall pleasing effect. It is not unusual for lumber selection for a single piece to take longer than its assembly. Most furniture factories stockpile and then pull parts as needed, resulting in utterly random color

an ancient mammalian tactic that aims to gather the maximum amount of sensory information during challenging tasks.

The assembly department is divided into two sections, cases and chairs. With their flat, straight, square components, cases are best assembled on flat, straight, square benches, and we have about a dozen. Each of the assemblers has a variety of shop-owned tools from which to choose, but it is a measure of the pride they take in their work that virtually all of them buy and use their own tools. Many use chisels and saws that have been in their families for generations, storing them in custom-made toolboxes that are glories of the woodworker's art.

Most chairs, on the other hand, are highly organic shapes—amalgams of curves and odd angles that refuse to lie still on traditional angular workbenches. In the chair-assembly department, craftsmen build and use a half-dozen customized workstations that are more like gloves, or perhaps wombs, encircling and holding the sweeps and arcs of chairs in a firm, protective embrace.

The lines of furniture production that diverge in assembly reunite in the sanding department. Sanding is the great, unappreciated secret

Opposite: Brenda Swett assembling a custom dresser. Even though most of the parts on a piece such as this are pre-cut, it still takes over a week to make.
Right: The wedge in an exposed tenon tightens the leg in the seat much the same way a handle is attached to an ax or hammer. Care must be taken to avoid splitting the seat.
Following pages: A Continuous Arm Chair ready for blanket wrapping and delivery.

of fine furniture. At our shop, an astounding one-third of total construction time is dedicated to sanding. Each piece of each item we make is sanded both before and after assembly, to a smoothness so fine that we use grits common in auto-body shops but almost never encountered in furniture factories.

Then comes the finishing room, where we apply our oil-and-wax finish. Like sanding, the work requires strenuous physical labor, but folks here thrive on a wonderful compensation: the moment that the first coat of 130-degree boiled linseed oil strikes the pale surface of cherry. At that instant, the wood's highlights and translucencies that no one up to now could have anticipated suddenly reveal themselves. The finishers say they never tire of that moment. I never have, either.

The final step is shipping, which most people regard as utilitarian, but doing it properly is an art in itself. Our passion for quality extends to installation and service; for many years, we have delivered and

Left: A pneumatic line sander is used to polish large surfaces, following the grain direction, before beeswax is applied. **Opposite:** Before receiving a floating panel, the inside edge of a dado is sanded.

installed nearly everything we build. We also retrieve, repair, and return any piece that may have been damaged through the years. This kind of attention is what gives us the temerity to offer a lifetime guarantee.

The most unusual aspect of our operation is not a department we have, but one we lack: quality control. Many factories employ whole teams of inspectors who ensure that the items produced meet certain minimum standards. This institutionalized distrust can demoralize production workers, and their aim can quickly become passing inspection rather than making the finest products possible. On our shop floor, every worker is also an inspector, empowered to pull a piece out of the line for repair or replacement if he or she spots a flaw. Giving each craftsman oversight responsibility means that problems are spotted and rectified more quickly. It also means that group pride, rather than fear, becomes the primary motivator.

Opposite: Marc LaBonte oversees the shipping effort. Here he blanket wraps before placing a Lolling Chair on the truck.
Right: Perhaps the simplest but most often used tool in the shop is a number two pencil. The adage "measure twice, cut once" becomes internalized quickly after a few mistakes.

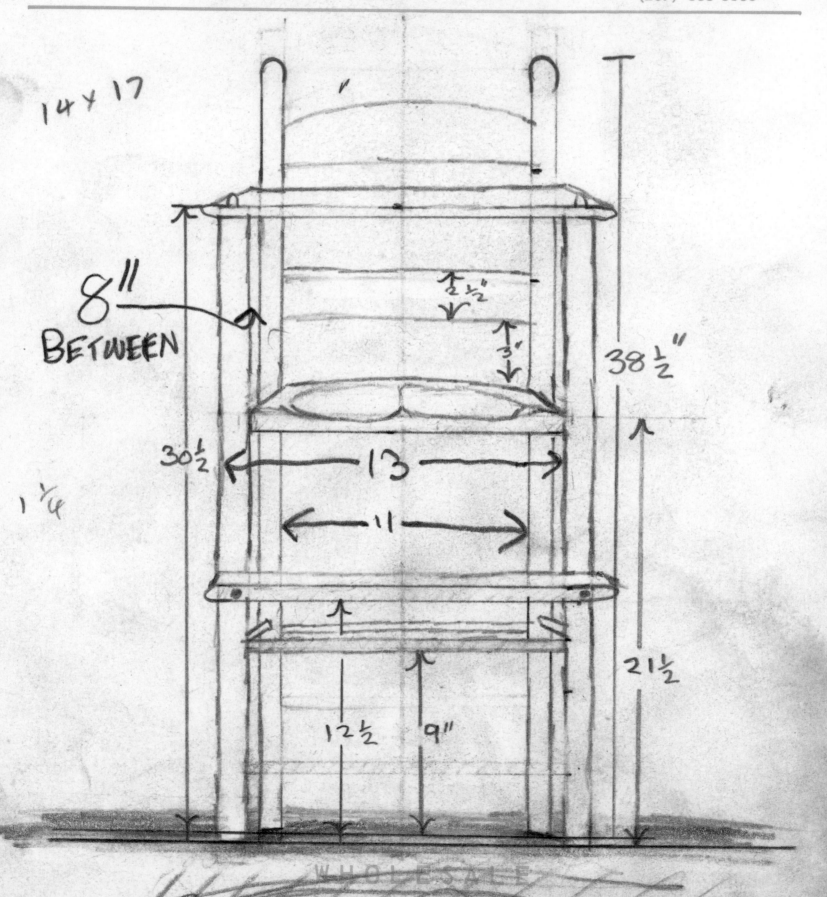

14 x 17

8" BETWEEN

2½"

3"

38½"

30½"

13

11

1¼

21½

12½   9"

ACKNOWLEDGMENTS

The art of working wood by hand reached its apogee in the mid-nineteenth century. The long dead joiners of that time remain my greatest teachers, for in their work (what we now call antiques) is to be found construction solutions and design truths for all who take the time to look. Their influence is heartfelt.

To these posthumous mentors I am indebted. To the many colleagues and employees who taught me through their manifest skills I am even more indebted. Each day we teach one another and are taught by one another. For this I give thanks.

This book owes much to Gretchen Kruysman, who, for several years, incessantly coaxed it into existence. Her enthusiasm and tenacity are especially appreciated. Brad Lemley, writer and friend, created order from chaos, helped me with my sometimes obtuse imagery, and put structure to my ramblings. He made less painful that hateful task of meeting a deadline. Most of the beautiful images in this book are the result of the photographic artistry of Paul Rocheleau. He sees in an instant and captures on film what I can only talk about. The design and layout of this book is the work of Tom Morgan, who, beginning with a box of several hundred photographs and images, built this tome. His mastery of two-dimensional space has the same integrity as the furniture shown.

Thanks to my long-suffering spouse, who supports me unfailingly. She is at once my chief critic and my inspiration. Special thanks to Dr. Clement Hiebert, who read this manuscript and offered many constructive comments. I am also grateful to Harry Fraser, who operates the company and affords me the freedom to dabble in other things, including the writing of this book. Lastly, I extend gratitude to the editors of Chronicle, who were as fussy as my doctoral committee so long ago.

Principal Photography

PAUL ROCHELEAU (pages: 5, 20, 27, 61, 62, 63, 70, 72, 78, 79, 82, 84–85, 89, 91, 96, 97, 99, 102, 110, 111, 112, 116–117, 118, 119, 121, 124, 126, 127, 130-131, 132, 133, 134, 135, 136–137, 140, 143, 145, 146, 147, 149, 150–151, 152, 153, 158–159, 160, 166, 167, 172, 173, 177, and 186)

CHRISTOPHER NAVIN (pages: 6-7, 8, 10, 18–19, 66, 67, 73, 80, 81, 83, 90, 98, 104, 120, 122, 141, 142, 144, 161, 162, 163, 169, 174, 176, 178, 179, 180, 181, 182, 183, 184–185, 187, 188, 189, and 192)

Contributing Photographers

Nathan Benn (page 101), Scott Dorrance (pages 92 and 171), Peter Macomber (cover; pages 115, 128–129, 131, 156, 168), Robert Reynolds (page 65), Jamie Salomon (pages 138–139), Lewis Tanner (pages 94–95), Stretch Tuemmler (pages 4, 86, 108–109, 123), Brian Vanden Brink (pages 12–13, 68–69, 164–165), Thomas Watkins (page 114)

Following page: A New Gloucester Rocker blanket wrapped and ready to be shipped. What isn't picked up by customers is usually delivered via special movers. This service bears the same imperative for excellence as the work itelf.

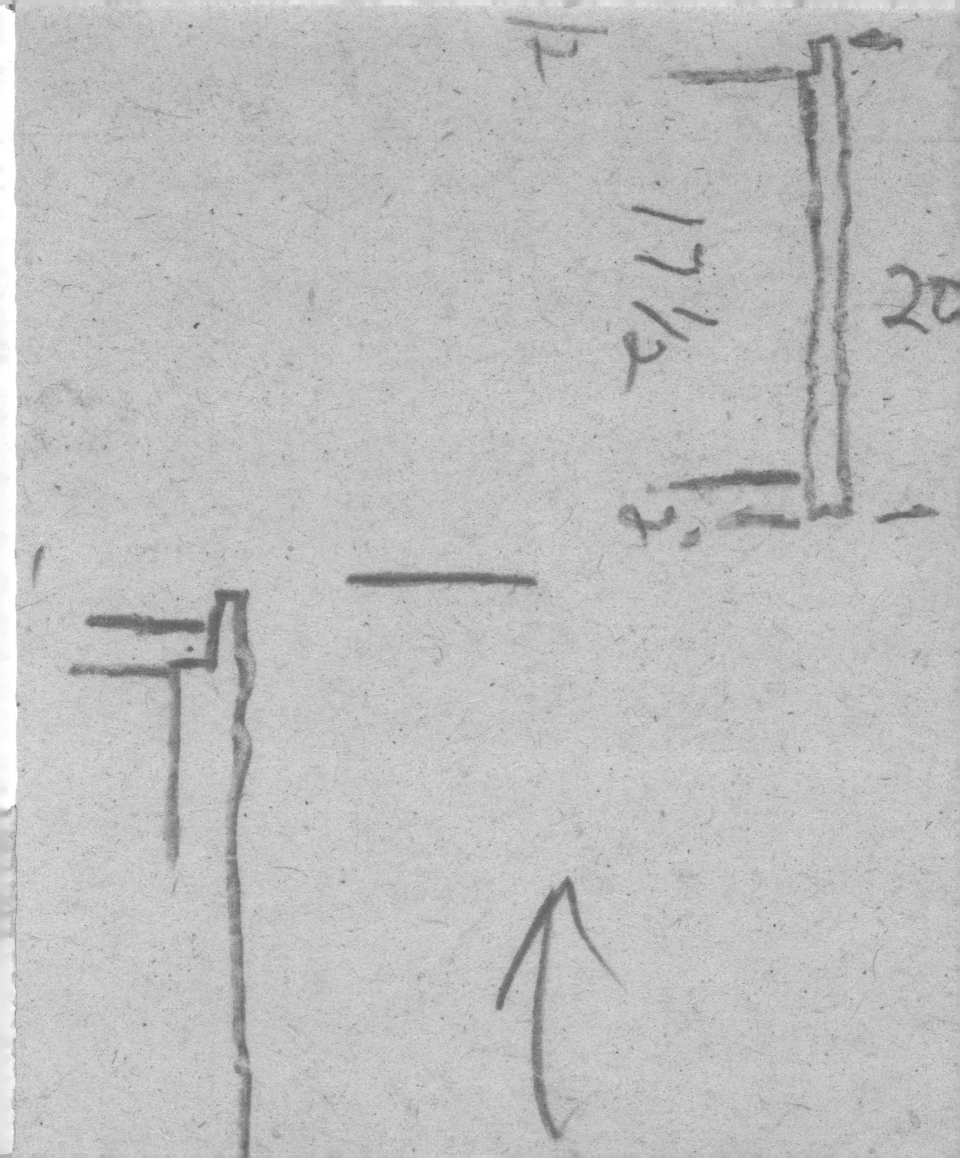

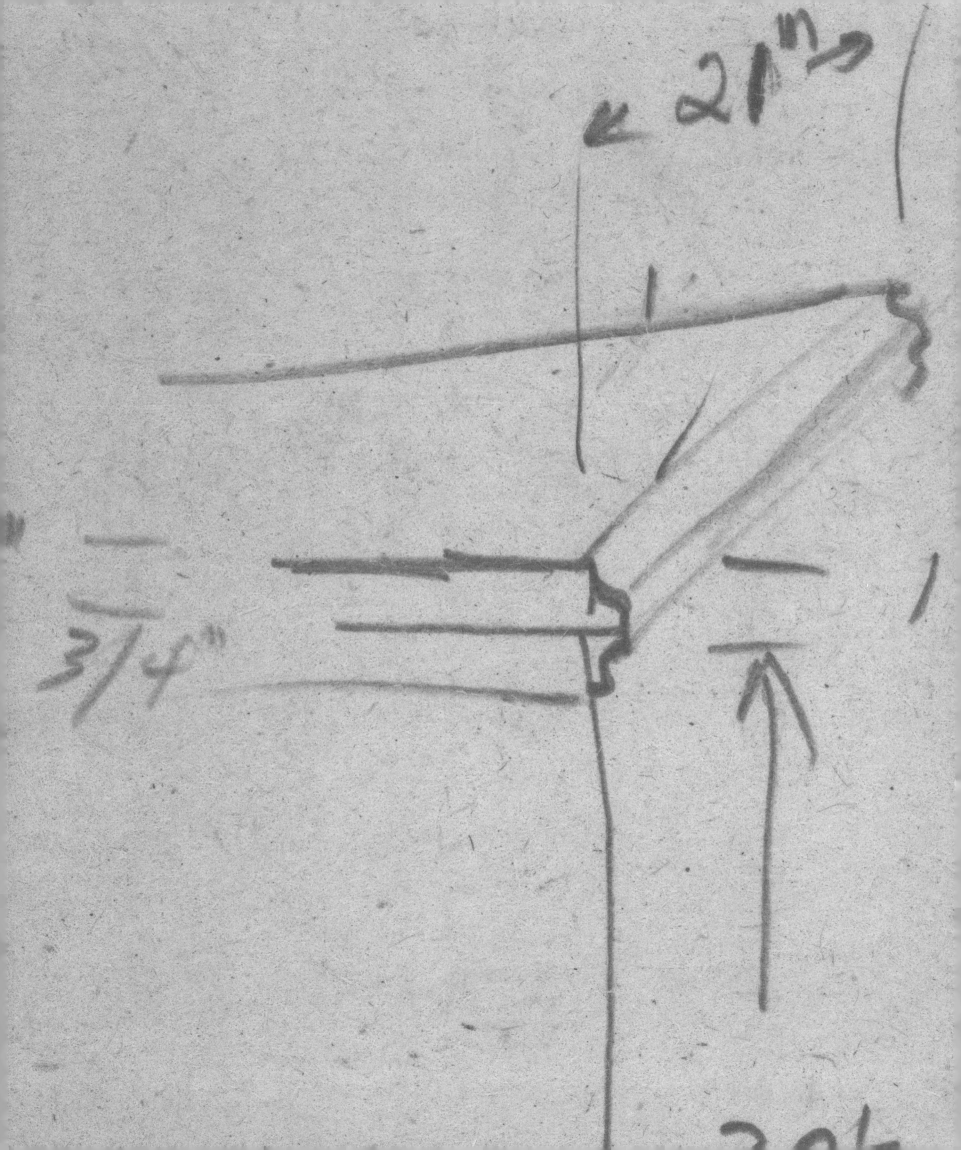